Developing Visual Basic Add-ins

Developing Visual Basic Add-ins

Steven Roman

O'REILLY®

Beijing · Cambridge · Köln · Paris · Sebastopol · Taipei · Tokyo

Developing Visual Basic Add-ins
by Steven Roman

Published by O'Reilly & Associates, Inc., 101 Morris Street, Sebastopol, CA 95472.

Editor: Ron Petrusha

Production Editor: Mary Anne Weeks Mayo

Printing History:

January 1999:	First Edition.

This book is printed on acid-free paper with 85% recycled content, 15% post-consumer waste. O'Reilly & Associates is committed to using paper with the highest recycled content available consistent with high quality.

ISBN: 1-56592-527-0   [4/99]

Table of Contents

Preface

A Visual Basic add-in is a software component that has complete *programmatic* access to the features of the Visual Basic development environment, officially known as the *Visual Basic Integrated Development Environment*, or VB IDE.

If you are like me, you are always looking for ways to perform certain tasks in the VB IDE in a more "natural" way, or simply wishing Microsoft had implemented a certain feature of the IDE in a different manner. In many cases, you can find a way to do what you want using an add-in.

Unfortunately, Microsoft has not brought the issue of creating VB add-ins to the forefront. Indeed, the VB documentation relegates a discussion of add-ins to the later part of Microsoft's *Visual Basic Component Tools Guide*. Moreover, the discussion is, shall we say, not as pedagogic as it might be. In addition, amazingly, the VB6 add-in documentation appears to be the same as the VB5 add-in documentation and thus doesn't reflect the changes made in VB6! (We will discuss these changes, however.)

In addition, the Microsoft Developer Network (MSDN) documentation suggests "The easiest way to create an add-in with Visual Basic is to start with the sample provided." This is clearly a cop out (which we will avoid).

When I first encountered add-ins under Visual Basic 4, the subject seemed completely shrouded in mystery. I wanted to make some alterations to the VB IDE, in particular to resize code windows automatically, to make keyboard navigation in the VB IDE more natural, and to add block commenting of code (a feature since implemented in VB5). I had to struggle for several days to arrive at an effective add-in.

The purpose of this little book is to help you create Visual Basic add-ins. It's intended for anyone who has at least a modest acquaintance with Visual Basic; you don't need to be an expert VB programmer.

I don't intend this book to be an encyclopedia on the subject. I cover the basics, show you how to write useful add-ins, give lots of simple coding examples, and provide you with all the necessary knowledge to delve into the many darker corners of the subject (which only the folks at Microsoft may fully understand).

I describe the add-in creation process for Visual Basic versions 5 and 6. Actually, the differences are relatively minor and relate to the initial setup and connection of the add-in rather than to the main programming features. In other words, the extensibility object models for VB5 and VB6 are essentially the same. (The VB6 model has one additional hidden object.)

Organization of This Book

Developing Visual Basic Add-ins consists of twelve chapters and two appendixes, and is divided into three parts.

Chapter 1, *Introduction*, provides a broad overview of the process of creating an add-in and examines why VB developers might want to create add-ins.

Part I, *Add-in Basics*, discusses the basic concepts you need to successfully develop an add-in of any kind. The process of developing an add-in is part mechanical and part creative; Chapter 2, *The Basic Components of an Add-in*, covers the mechanics of creating an add-in—the basic steps you need to develop an add-in of any kind that works in the Visual Basic integrated development environment. Chapter 3, *Object Models*, focuses on the concept of an object model and on the basic VBA language constructs you need in order to work with objects. If you have experience working with object models and handling objects, you can either skip this chapter or browse through it very quickly. Chapter 4, *Menus and Toolbars*, shows how to make your add-in accessible from the VB menu system or from a VB toolbar. Chapter 5, *Debugging Add-ins*, discusses some of the special considerations involved with debugging and testing an add-in.

When developing add-ins, the creative aspect comes in when working with the VB IDE's object model either to change the way the VB IDE operates or to add some new functionality it currently lacks. Consequently, Part II, *The Extensibility Model*, covers the objects of the Visual Basic extensibility model and the access they give to the VB IDE. Chapter 6, *Overview of the Object Model*, provides a general look at the VB IDE object model. Chapters 7 through 12 then examine individual objects in the object model, along with their properties, methods, events, collections, and child objects.

Finally, Part III of the book contains two appendixes. Appendix A, *Built-in Command Bar Controls*, lists the command-bar controls you can access from your applications. Appendix B, *Face IDs*, displays the complete set of button images stored with VB, along with the face ID you need to display the image on a toolbar.

Obtaining the Sample Programs

The sample programs presented in the book are available online and can be freely downloaded from our web site at *http://www.oreilly.com/catalog/vbaddin/*.

Conventions in This Book

Throughout this book, I use the following typographic conventions:

`Constant width`

indicates a language construct such as a language statement, a constant, or an expression. Lines of code also appear in constant width, as do function and method prototypes, and variable and parameter names.

Italic

represents intrinsic and application-defined functions and procedures, modules, the names of system elements such as directories and files, and Internet resources such as web documents and email addresses. New terms are also italicized when they are first introduced.

`Constant width italic`

in prototypes or command syntax indicates replaceable parameter names. In text, it indicates variable names.

 If you see an icon featured in the margin (see left), it denotes that the text that follows pertains to whatever version is indicated.

How to Contact Us

We have tested and verified all the information in this book to the best of our ability, but you may find that features have changed (or even that we have made mistakes!). Please let us know about any errors you find, as well as your suggestions for future editions, by writing to:

O'Reilly & Associates, Inc.
101 Morris Street
Sebastopol, CA 95472
1-800-998-9938 (in the United States or Canada)
1-707-829-0515 (international/local)
1-707-829-0104 (fax)

You can also send messages electronically. To be put on our mailing list or to request a catalog, send email to:

> *nuts@oreilly.com*

To ask technical questions or comment on the book, send email to:

> *bookquestions@oreilly.com*

O'Reilly now has a Visual Basic resource center, located at *vb.oreilly.com*. The web site is intended as a resource for the entire Visual Basic community and features original articles and a discussion forum devoted to general VB progarmming issues. As mentioned previously, this book has a web site (*http://www.oreilly.com/ catalog/vbaddin/*) from which you can link to any future errata pages and other news and information.

Acknowledgments

This is the third book that I've written with O'Reilly & Associates, and I would like to again express my thanks to Ron Petrusha, editor at O'Reilly, for another outstanding job. His help was invaluable as usual.

Thanks also goes to David Jezak, for his helpful comments and suggestions for this book.

Lastly, thanks to the production staff at O'Reilly & Associates, including Mary Anne Weeks Mayo, project manager and copyeditor; Jane Ellin, Melanie Wang, Sarah Jane Shangraw, and Sheryl Avruch for quality control; Ruth Rautenberg for the index; Mike Sierra for Frame tools support; Rob Romano for illustrations; Kathleen Wilson for the backcover; and Edie Freedman for designing another memorable cover.

1

Introduction

A Visual Basic add-in is a software component that has complete *programmatic* access to the features of the Visual Basic development environment, officially known as the Visual Basic integrated development environment, or IDE. Visual Basic comes with several add-ins created by the Microsoft VB programming group. Add-ins can range from simple components that, for example, clear the Immediate window, to complex components such as the Microsoft Class Builder Utility, which assists in creating and maintaining multiple classes and their relationships.

The Add-in Creation Process

The process of creating an add-in is actually fairly easy to follow if we think about the more or less common-sense steps that are required to prepare an add-in for use. This does not include adding functionality (that is, features) to the add-in, which is the major part of add-in creation. To help avoid confusion, note that there is a distinction between the add-in *programmer* (that's us) and the add-in *user*, who is also programming in the VB environment.

1. *Registering the add-in*

   As with most Windows applications, we must provide a means for VB to get general information about our add-in. This information includes the kind (DLL or EXE) and location of the add-in's executable file, as well as type information about the add-in's public class (this statement will make more sense as you read on). This information is provided by registering the add-in in the system registry.

2. *Providing a method for add-in activation*

   An add-in can be *activated*—that is, executed (for an EXE) or loaded (for a DLL)—either during a VB session or when VB is started. The most common way for a user to activate an add-in is by using the Add-In Manager. We must therefore instruct the Add-In Manager to include ours in its list of available add-ins. In VB5, this is done by placing a line in the *vbaddin.ini* file, which resides in the Windows directory. In VB6, the process is made a bit simpler by using the Add-In Designer.

Alternatively, add-ins can be activated programmatically by other add-ins. This is the basis for VB's Add-In Toolbar, which is an add-in whose sole function is to activate other add-ins. As the name implies, the Add-In Toolbar displays a toolbar with buttons for each installed add-in, as well as a button for installing or removing additional add-ins.

3. *Connecting the add-in*

   Finally, we must provide VB with a way to give our add-in programmatic access to the VB IDE. After all, this is the whole point of an add-in. This process is properly referred to as *connecting the add-in* (although some may use this term more loosely to refer to the activation process as well). There is a slight difference in the way this is done in VB5 and VB6, but the principle is the same in both cases.

Connecting an add-in is by far the most interesting portion of add-in setup. To understand the process, we need to discuss the VB Extensibility object model.

The VB Extensibility Object Model

An add-in gains programmatic access to the Visual Basic IDE by gaining access to the *Microsoft Visual Basic Extensibility Object Model*, also called the *VB IDE object model*. The VBIDE object library, which contains the information about the objects in the VBIDE model, is named *vb5ext.olb* in Visual Basic 5.0 and *vb6ext.olb* in Visual Basic 6.0. However, these models are essentially the same.

Simply put, an object model is a collection of interrelated objects that have *properties* that can be set and retrieved, and that can be manipulated through *actions*, also called *methods*. Of course, the objects in an object model are intended to represent the "objects" in the application that is associated with the model.

Microsoft uses object models to represent the objects in many of its applications. For instance, the Microsoft Word object model contains almost 200 different object types. There is a Document object that represents a Word document and a Paragraph object that represents a paragraph within a document. There is also a Documents collection object that "holds" all the Document objects that represent the currently open Word documents. (For more on the Word object model, see my book *Learning Word Programming*, also published by O'Reilly & Associates.)

To illustrate the notion of properties and methods: the Document object has a property called FullName that gives the full path and filename of the document and a property called Content that gives the contents of the document. It also has a method called Close that closes the document and a method called PrintPreview that places the document in print preview mode. (The Document object alone has a total of 112 properties and 58 methods!)

Microsoft provides over a dozen different object models for its Office application suite and related products. These include object models for Word, Excel, Access, DAO (Data Access Objects), Outlook, PowerPoint, Binder, Graph, Forms, VBA, VB, ASP (Active Server Pages), and more. Of course, this book's focus is on the VB IDE object model, which has about 50 objects.

One of the most important characteristics of object models is their hierarchical structure. Put more simply, some objects can be considered *children* of other objects. This parent-child relationship creates a hierarchical structure within the model. For instance, in the Word object model, each Document object has a child Paragraphs collection object that holds all the Paragraph objects for the paragraphs in that document. Thus, we would say that the Paragraphs collection object is a child of the Document object and that Document is a parent of Paragraphs.

Accessing an Object Model

Most object models have a single "top" object that is either directly or indirectly the parent of all other objects in the model. This object provides an entry point to the entire object model (although sometimes lower-level objects are directly accessible as well). In most cases (such as for Word, Access, Excel, and PowerPoint), the top object is called *Application*, since it represents the application itself. Indeed, in the VB4 Extensibility model, the top object is the Application object. However, in the VB5 and VB6 Extensibility models, the top object is called the VBE object.

We should clarify one point of possible confusion. An object model is just a blueprint for the objects and their relationships to one another. To actually use an object model, we must first create at least one object. For instance, the following code creates the top object in the Word object model. In other words, it starts Microsoft Word and returns a reference to the Application object that represents this instance of Word:

```
Dim wrd As Word.Application
Set wrd = New Word.Application
```

An alternative you may have seen is:

```
Dim wrd as Word.Application
Set wrd = CreateObject("Word.Application")
```

We can now programmatically create a new Word document, for instance, by writing:

```
Dim doc as Document
Set doc = Wrd.Documents.Add
```

All this is very elegant, and allows us to programmatically control, or *automate*, Microsoft Word from within another application. A similar approach is used to automate Excel, PowerPoint, Access, and other applications.

This is precisely want we want to do with the VB IDE object model, but there is one rather significant difference in approach. Namely, we don't create an object of type VBE. Instead, VB itself creates the object when we start a new VB session. The problem is how to get a reference to that object!

The solution provided by Microsoft is quite simple.

VB5 In VB5, we are required to implement a certain interface called the IDTExtensibility interface. This amounts simply to adding this line to a class module:

```
Implements IDTExtensibility
```

Briefly, an *interface* is a collection of methods. The IDTExtensibility interface contains four methods (described in the next section) defined by Microsoft. The above line of code says to VB that we will implement these methods; that is, we will write the code that is executed when the methods are invoked (in this case by VB). In fact, VB provides us with code shells in which we can place this code. Thus, in effect, VB turns these methods into *events*.

As we will see, the OnConnection method of the IDTExtensibility interface, which appears to us as a VB event, has a parameter called *VBInst* of type Object. When the add-in is activated, say by the user through the Add-In Manager (or through code from another add-in), VB itself points this parameter to the current instance of the VBE object; that is, to the instance of the VBE object that refers to the current instance of the VB IDE. All we need to do as add-in programmers is grab this parameter, with a line such as:

```
Set oVBE = VBInst
```

where *oVBE* is a global object variable. We now have access to the entire VBE object model through our variable *oVBE*, which points to the top object in the model.

VB6 VB6 also supports the IDTExtensibility interface, probably for backward compatibility only, and so we can still use this interface for connecting add-ins. However, in VB6, the preferred method is to add a special class called an *Add-In Class* to the add-in project. This class provides access to the methods of an interface called AddinInstance. This interface has the same methods as IDTExtensibility, along with three additional methods (as we will see). In particular, it includes the OnConnection method. However, in this case, the method returns a parameter called *Application* that points to the top level VBE object, so we write:

```
Set oVBE = Application
```

The reason for the change of name is that add-ins can (either now or in the future) be used in development environments other than Visual Basic (such as Visual C++ and Microsoft Office), so the object returned by connecting an add-in may not always be VBE.

In any case, as you can see, the underlying principle behind add-in connection is the same in VB5 and VB6, but the implementation is a bit different.

In either case, the add-in project becomes an *automation client*, using the Automation objects of the VB IDE object model provided by VB, which is therefore the *automation server*. This is ActiveX Automation in action.

Connecting an Add-in

Let's take a closer look at the issue of connecting an add-in.

The main design feature of an add-in is a class module that exists specifically for the purpose of providing VB with a way to pass a reference to the VBE object for the current session of VB.

In particular, every add-in must have a class module we will refer to as the Connect class. This class module is customarily named Connect, but this isn't a requirement. The procedure for creating this class is different for VB5 than for VB6.

VB5 In VB5, we simply add a class module to the add-in project. Let's call this class module the Connect class. The Instancing property of the Connect class must be set to MultiUse, so that Connect class objects can be created by Visual Basic, which can then invoke the methods of the IDTExtensibility interface (such as OnConnection). Note that the Instancing property must be set to MultiUse since a single add-in may be used by more than one instance of VB, which means that more than one instance of the Connect class might be created at the same time.

Within the Connect class module, we are required to implement *each* of the IDTExtensibility interface's four methods:

- OnAdInsUpdate
- OnConnection
- OnDisconnection
- OnStartupComplete

This is done by placing the line:

```
Implements IDTExtensibility
```

in the Declarations section of the Connect class. This code tells VB that we will implement the methods of the IDTExtensibility interface and asks VB to provide us with code shells for the methods. (Of course, it also tells VB to call those methods at the appropriate time.)

For the present discussion, the most important of these methods is OnConnection. When we start the add-in activation process, for instance by using the Add-In Manager to load the add-in, VB does the following:

1. It uses the information in the *vbaddin.ini* file (in particular, the ProgID, discussed in the section "The Add-in Project Itself" in Chapter 2, *The Basic Components of an Add-in*) to find the information about the add-in that is registered in the system registry. This information includes the location of the add-in's executable (DLL or EXE).

2. It activates (starts) the add-in and creates a Connect object from the add-in's Connect class. (The name of the Connect class is also given in the *vbaddin.ini* file.)

3. It then executes the OnConnection method we have implemented for this Connect class object, passing in a reference to the VBE object for the current session of VB.

The (VB5) syntax of the OnConnection method is:

```
Private Sub IDTExtensibility_OnConnection( _
        ByVal VBInst As Object, _
        ByVal ConnectMode As vbext_ConnectMode, _
        ByVal AddInInst As VBIDE.AddIn, _
        custom() As Variant)
```

Note the parameter *VBInst*. This is filled by VB with a reference to the VBE object for the current instance of VB. This parameter is colloquially referred to as the current instance of VB, although the absolutely correct object-oriented terminology would be "a parameter that refers to the current instance of the VBE class for the currently running instance of the VB IDE."

Accordingly, the first thing that we should do in the OnConnection method is to save the value of the parameter *VBInst*, because once the OnConnection method terminates, the *VBInst* parameter is no longer valid. This is done by declaring a module-level or global-level public variable:

```
Public oVBE As VBIDE.VBE
```

and then including the following line in the OnConnection method:

```
Set oVBE = VBInst
```

After all, this reference is our only entrée to the VB IDE object model, and we don't want to lose it!

Since it is Visual Basic that calls OnConnection and the three other methods of the IDTExtensibility interface, they appear to the add-in simply as events. This explains the following quotation from the OnConnection topic in the Microsoft help file:

> While the OnConnection method is a method to the IDTExtensibility interface, to you as a Visual Basic programmer it acts and behaves like an event. In other words, when an add-in is connected to the Visual Basic IDE, either through the Add-In Manager dialog box or another add-in, any code in the OnConnection method automatically occurs, just as if it were an event procedure.

VB6 | VB6 attempts to make the connection process simpler (although it really isn't that complicated in the first place) by providing a special designer called the Addin Class. The Addin Class designer can be thought of as a normal class module together with a dialog that is used to help design the add-in. The class name for the designer can be optionally changed to Connect, but the designer's Public property must be set to True. The Addin Class designer *implicitly* adds the code:

```
Implements AddInInstance
```

to the project. Thus, we don't need to add this line. Also, unlike the VB5 case, we only need to implement those methods of the AddInInstance interface we actually use.

The OnConnection method has a slightly different syntax in VB6 than in VB5. The VB6 syntax is:

```
Private Sub AddinInstance_OnConnection( _
    ByVal Application As Object, _
    ByVal ConnectMode As AddInDesignerObjects.ext_ConnectMode, _
    ByVal AddInInst As Object, _
    custom() As Variant)
```

The main thing to notice is that the parameter *VBInst* has been replaced by the parameter *Application*. However, the *Application* parameter still points to the top VBE object, so its use is identical with that of VB5's *VBInst* parameter. In particular, we declare a module- or global-level public variable:

```
Public oVBE As VBIDE.VBE
```

and then include the following line in the OnConnection method:

```
Set oVBE = Application
```

Note also that VB6 does not require the *vbaddin.ini* file as VB5 does. Instead, the Add-In Manager looks directly to the Windows registry for the necessary information. The Addin Class designer's dialog box is used to register the required information. We discuss this in more detail in the section "The Add-In Manager..." in Chapter 2.

What Can an Add-in Do?

Once an add-in is connected, the easy part—that is, the noncreative part—is done. The add-in now has complete programmatic access to the VB IDE object model, through the *oVBE* object variable.

Even though the VB IDE object model is relatively small as Microsoft object models go, with only 51 objects and about 260 properties and 170 methods, it is still quite substantial, and we will spend the majority of our time discussing this model. Unfortunately, the VBIDE model is one of the worst documented models in Microsoft's arsenal. In fact, for many objects and their properties and methods, there is essentially no documentation at all! Nevertheless, there is enough documentation on the major portions of the object model to create useful add-ins.

Even without discussing the specifics of the VB IDE object model, we can get a pretty good idea of what add-ins can do.

Controlling the User Interface

The VB IDE object model has objects that allow us to extend the IDE user interface itself. This is the visual component of the IDE. For instance, we can:

- Add new menus or toolbars to the VB IDE or add new commands to existing menus and toolbars
- Open, close, or change the size of windows in the IDE
- Determine which portion of code is currently displayed in a given window; we can also get or set the code that is currently selected

Controlling VB Projects

The VB IDE object model gives us control over VB projects. For instance, we can:

- Remove a project from the IDE
- Start a new project
- Save or compile a project
- React to the loading or unloading of a given project
- Get or set various properties of a given project, such as the project's name, the type of the project (Standard EXE, ActiveX EXE, ActiveX DLL, etc.), whether the project has been saved since the last time it was edited, and so on
- Add or remove individual components from the project

Controlling VB Forms

When we design a form, ActiveX control, or ActiveX document within the VB IDE, we are actually working within a special window referred to as a *designer*.

The VB IDE object model allows us to manipulate designer windows—that is, to design a form through code. In particular, we can add or remove controls from a form, and change the properties of controls. (Note that unlike Version 5 of VB, Version 6 has a feature that allows forms to be designed though code, and controls to be added or removed dynamically, without making use of the extensibility model and VB add-ins.)

Responding to Events in the VB IDE

When the VB user manipulates the IDE through the usual means, VB fires various events. These are not the same events that are fired while a VB application is running in response to user interaction. Rather, these events are fired during Visual Basic's runtime—that is, during design time.

The Visual Basic IDE's events are divided into seven groups within the VB IDE object model:

- CommandBar events (Command bars are menus and toolbars)
- File Control events
- Reference events
- Selected VB Controls events
- VB Components events
- VB Controls events
- VB Projects events

For instance, there are three VB Components events: ItemAdded, ItemRemoved, and ItemRenamed, and we may write code to respond to any of these three events. There is only one Command Bar event—the Click event. Of course, this event fires when a VB menu or toolbar command is selected.

Controlling VB Code

The VB IDE object model also gives us access to the actual code in a VB project. We can add, delete, or change code, as well as search for specific strings. We can also insert code from an external file.

Controlling Add-ins

Finally, the VBIDE model gives us limited control over add-ins themselves. In particular, we can connect and disconnect add-ins using code. As we have said, this is the basis for the Add-In Toolbar that is included with VB itself.

The Visual Basic Add-in Template

You may have noticed that Visual Basic comes with a built-in template for creating add-ins. This template can be accessed by selecting New from the Visual Basic File menu and choosing the Add-In icon in the New Project dialog box.

Frankly, the code that is automatically inserted by choosing the Add-In template seems to me to be both overly complicated and unduly confusing. Accordingly, I don't use this template. In fact, one of the main purposes of Chapter 2 of this book is to create a simple add-in template (or add-in code shell) that can serve as a starting place for building useful add-ins. Indeed, we will use this shell throughout the book as we explore the features of the VBE extensibility object model.

I

Add-in Basics

2

The Basic Components of an Add-in

In an overall sense, creating a meaningful add-in is a two-part process. The first part is to create the *add-in shell*, which is everything except the *features* of the add-in. In other words, the add-in shell is a fully functional add-in, but it does nothing. This is the routine part. The second part is to write the code that implements the features of the add-in. This is the creative part.

As we have discussed, creating an add-in shell involves three steps:

1. Registering the add-in in the system registry

2. Providing a means for add-in activation

3. Connecting the add-in

In this chapter, we take a look at these steps. During this process, we will create the code that is required of essentially every add-in; that is, an add-in code shell. This add-in code shell can be used as the starting point for building functional add-ins, as well as for experimenting with add-in code. At the end of the chapter, we will put together all the pieces of our add-in shell. This is a good time for you to create your own add-in shell to use to experiment with the code in the remaining portion of the book.

The Add-in Project Itself

Of course, the very first step in creating an add-in is to create a new project. Add-ins can be ActiveX DLLs or ActiveX EXEs. The main difference between the two is that a DLL runs in the same address space (the same process) as the application that invokes it, whereas an EXE runs in its own address space (process). For this reason, a DLL add-in is referred to as an *in-process* add-in, and an EXE add-in is referred to as an *out-of-process* add-in.

Not only does an in-process add-in provide faster response than an out-of-process add-in, but an in-process add-in has greater access to the current instance of the VB IDE, since it doesn't need to break down the process barriers that are built into Windows. Thus, add-ins should be in-process unless there is a compelling reason to do otherwise. For example, as the Microsoft documentation points out, we might want to create an ActiveX EXE add-in if that add-in will also function as a standalone application that does something useful apart from its role as an add-in. Another possibility is that the add-in may reside on a remote PC, in which case it must be an EXE. Accordingly, our add-in code shell will be in-process.

After starting a new ActiveX DLL project, its properties should be set in the Project Properties dialog box, as shown in Figure 2-1. Here we double-check that the project type is ActiveX DLL and set the project name and description. Since our basic add-in doesn't require any startup code, we set the Startup Object to (None).

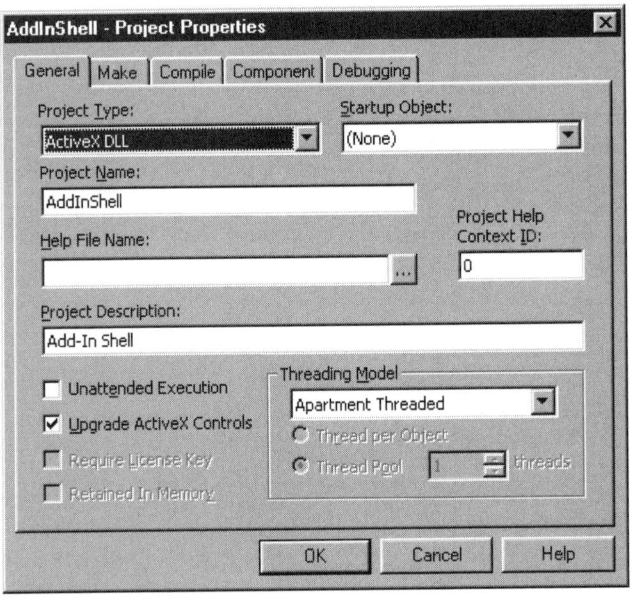

Figure 2-1. Add-in project properties

It's important to note that the projectname and the Connect class name (discussed next) play an important role in identifying the add-in. In particular, the project name followed by a period and the name of the Connect class:

```
ProjectName.ConnectClassName
```

is called the *Programmatic Identifier*, or ProgID, for the add-in. For instance, the ProgID for our add-in shell is:

```
AddInShell.Connect
```

We will see several places in which this ProgID is used. The point I want to make now is that, since the ProgID is used for identification of the add-in on *any* system on which it may be used, and since the Connect class name of most add-ins is Connect, it's important to choose a unique project name. (For instance, you might want to incorporate your company's name into the add-in's project name.)

Adding the Connect Class

Once the project is created, we need to add our Connect class.

VB5   Recall that, in order to gain access to the VBE object for the currently running instance of the VB IDE, we need to implement the IDTExtensibility interface. In Visual Basic, interfaces can be implemented only within class modules. Accordingly, every add-in requires a class module, referred to as the Connect class for the add-in. As mentioned earlier, it's customary (but not mandatory) to give this class module the name Connect. Also, we must set its Instancing property to MultiUse so that VB can create multiple Connect class objects in case our add-in is used by multiple instances of the VB IDE at the same time.

Thus, the next step in creating our add-in is to add a class module to the project, rename it Connect, and set its Instancing property to MultiUse. (If the project already has a class module, just rename it Connect.) Then add the following line to the Declarations section of the module:

```
Implements IDTExtensibility
```

As mentioned earlier, we are required by VB to implement each of the four methods of the IDTExtensibility interface, even if it means simply adding a comment to each method. (According to Microsoft's documentation, each method must contain at least a comment in order to prevent it from being removed upon compilation. I have been able to successfully compile add-ins without adding comments to an otherwise empty method of the IDTExtensibility interface, but I would never consider doing so in an add-in intended for distribution. *Caveat scriptor.*)

You should next select the IDTExtensibility item in the Objects drop-down list box, as shown in Figure 2-2. The Procedures drop-down list box will then contain the names of the interface's four methods. Select each method in turn and add a comment mark to the code shell, as the following example shows:

```
Private Sub IDTExtensibility_OnAddInsUpdate(custom() _
    As Variant)
'
End Sub
```

(Later, we will replace these comment marks by some additional code, at least for some of these methods. In any case, we're covered; we've implemented all the required methods.)

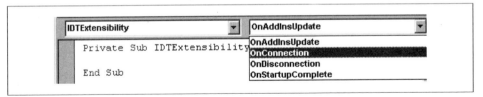

Figure 2-2. Implementing the IDTExtensibility interface

VB6   Under VB6, we add an Addin Class designer to the add-in project. This is a two-step process. First, select the Components item on the Project menu. Then select the Designer tab, shown in Figure 2-3. On the Designers tab, check the Addin Class designer and hit the OK button. (Incidentally, the help documentation incorrectly refers to this entry as the AddInDesigner object.)

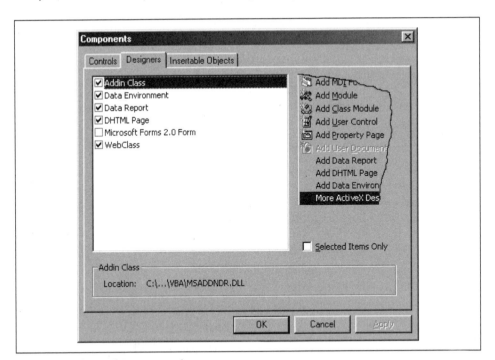

Figure 2-3. The VB6 Designers tab

Next, choose the Add Addin Class menu item from the Projects menu. (Again, the help documentation incorrectly refers to this menu item as AddInDesigner.) This places a new designer in the project. Using the Properties window, the designer's name can be (optionally) changed to Connect, but its Public property must be changed to True. This designer implicitly adds the code:

```
Implements AddInInstance
```

to the project. (Thus, we don't need to add this line.) We can then implement the desired methods of the AddInInstance interface.

To do so, open the Connect object's code module and select the AddInInstance item in the Objects drop-down list box, as shown in Figure 2-4. In VB6, you don't need to implement all the events in AddInInstance.

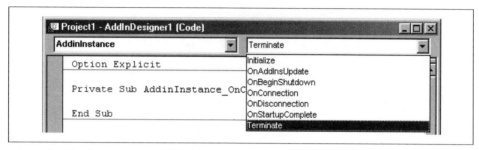

Figure 2-4. Implementing the AddinInstance interface

Registering an Add-in

As we have discussed, in order for VB to activate the add-in, it must have a way to locate the add-in's executable file (DLL or EXE). VB must also have a way to get information about the public Connect class for the add-in, so it can create a Connect object and call its OnConnection method. To get this information, the add-in must be registered in the system registry.

Fortunately, the very act of compiling an add-in causes it to be registered in the registry. This is the end of the story if the add-in is being run on the same PC upon which it was compiled. However, if we create an add-in and give or sell it to others, we must provide a way to register the add-in on the user's machine.

An ActiveX EXE add-in is automatically registered when it's run, so there are no problems here. In addition, an EXE can be registered without executing it by appending the **/regserver** switch to the command line. For instance, if the add-in's executable is *AddInShell.exe*, then running:

```
AddInShell.exe /regserver
```

from the Windows Run dialog registers the add-in without running it.

To register an in-process add-in, Microsoft provides a utility called *Regsvr32.exe* (which usually resides in the Windows System directory, but you can also find it at *ftp.microsoft.com/softlib/mslfiles/*). All we need to do is run:

```
Regsvr32 d:\AddIn\AddInShell.dll
```

to register the add-in, or:

```
Regsvr32 /u d:\AddIn\AddInShell.dll
```

to unregister it. (Note the complete path name for the DLL.) RegSvr32 issues a confirmation message upon success, or a rather cryptic error message if there is a problem. For instance, an error message similar to the one shown in Figure 2-5 appears when RegSvr32 can't find the DLL, probably because we have either misspelled its name or used the incorrect path.

Figure 2-5. An example RegSvr32 error message

Of course, if the add-in is distributed, we probably don't want to make our customers run RegSvr32, so this step should be incorporated into the setup program for the add-in. This also applies to creating a reference to the add-in in the *vbaddin.ini* file, which we discuss in "The Add-In Manager..." section later in this chapter. (The procedure for doing these things depends on how you create the setup program for your add-in. When using the setup toolkit that comes with VB, it's necessary to edit the setup toolkit's code. See the chapter on distributing applications in the *Visual Basic Programmer's Guide* for more details. If you use a third-party setup program, such as InstallShield's Express2, you need to refer to the documentation for that program.)

Referencing the VBIDE Object Library

In order for our add-in to recognize the objects in the VBIDE object library, we need to set a reference to this library. This is done from the References dialog box (under the Project menu) shown in Figure 2-6, by selecting the Microsoft Visual Basic 5.0 Extensibility or Microsoft Visual Basic 6.0 Extensibility reference, depending on your version of Visual Basic.

Notice also that we have referenced the Microsoft Office Object Library. This library contains objects for the menus and toolbars in the VB IDE (as well as the Microsoft Office application's visual interfaces). Any add-in that manipulates the menus or toolbars of the VB IDE (and most add-ins do) will need a reference to this object model, which we discuss at length in Chapter 4, *Menus and Toolbars.*

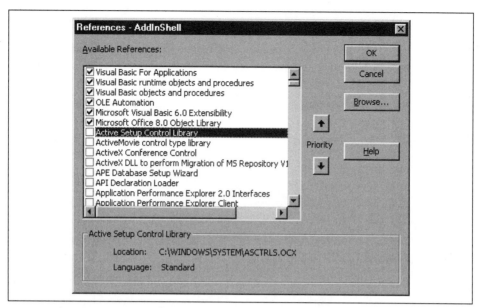

Figure 2-6. References for the add-in

How the Registry Is Used

It's interesting and informative to take a look at some of the data that is actually stored in the registry when an add-in is registered. (This applies to registering other types of ActiveX applications as well.)

As we have said, the registry supplies two key pieces of information about the add-in: the name and location of the executable file (DLL or EXE), and information about the Connect class for the add-in. The latter information is called *type information* and is contained in a *type library*, also called an *object library*. Type libraries are often a part of the executable file itself, as is the case with an add-in.

We should remark that the registry supplies other information of a more technical nature. For instance, it contains information about how to handle cross-process calls for an out-of-process add-in (this is called *marshalling information*).

Figure 2-7 shows a portion of the registry entries for our add-in shell. The three branches of HKEY_CLASSES_ROOT shown come from different locations in the registry, but we have brought them together for ease of viewing.

The first branch is headed by a key whose name is the ProgID of the add-in. The value of this key is the description of the Connect class that appears in the Add-In Manager. For instance, the Add-In Manager displays a checkbox labeled Add-In Shell for our add-in. We discuss how to set this description, which defines how

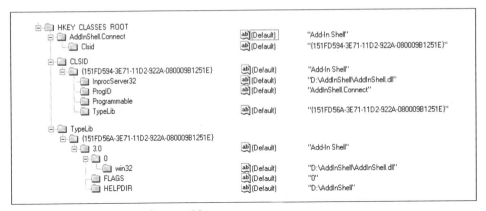

Figure 2-7. Registry entries for an add-in

the add-in is identified to the end user, when we talk about the Add-In Manager a bit later, but we should emphasize two important points in this regard now:

- If we don't supply a description of the Connect class, VB places the ProgID in the Add-In Manager. Since AddInShell.Connect isn't a very friendly name, it behooves us to supply a Connect class description.

- Contrary to what we might have expected, the Add-In Manager doesn't display the project name or description for an add-in. Instead, it displays the name (i.e., ProgID) or description (if present) of the add-in's Connect class to the user. This isn't unreasonable, since the Connect class is the only portion of the add-in that is public (that is, visible to other applications).

VB uses the ProgID (which it retrieves from the *vbaddin.ini* file, for instance) to get the *class ID* (CLSID) for the add-in. It can then look under the CLSID branch of the registry (the second branch in Figure 2-7) to find the `InprocServer32` key (short for 32-bit in-process server), whose value is the complete path and filename of the add-in's DLL. This is how VB finds the add-in. (An EXE add-in has a key named `LocalServer32` in place of `InProcServer32`.)

In addition, the CLSID branch of the registry has a `TypeLib` key whose value is another ID number, called a *library ID*, or LIBID. The third branch of the registry shown in Figure 2-7 lists all LIBIDs known to the system. Under the entry for our add-in's type library, VB can find the name and location of that library. In this case, it's just the DLL itself. In addition, there is a key that gives the version number of the type library and the location of the help file for the type library, if one exists.

The Add-In Manager and the Add-In Toolbar

There are basically two ways to activate an add-in: one is through the Add-In Manager and the other is programmatically, from another add-in. As we mentioned earlier, the Add-In Toolbar is an example of an add-in that activates other add-ins.

The Add-In Manager

The most common way to activate an add-in is to use the Add-In Manager. By reading the *vbaddin.ini* file or (in the case of VB6) the registry, this utility, whose dialog box is shown in Figure 2-8, simply provides a list of add-ins. The Add-In Manager can be invoked at any time from the Add-Ins menu.

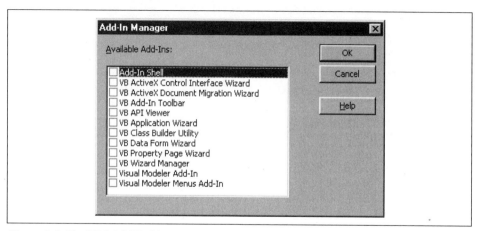

Figure 2-8. The VB5 Add-In Manager

VB5 In the VB5 version of the dialog, any add-in whose checkbox is selected is activated automatically when VB starts. The user can also activate an add-in at any time by invoking the Add-In Manager and checking the add-in's checkbox. Note that the checkbox remains checked after VB is closed, so if the user doesn't want the add-in to start automatically the next time VB is started, the checkbox must be unchecked before closing VB.

VB6 In the VB6 version of the dialog, which is shown in Figure 2-9, we begin by selecting a particular add-in. The Load Behavior group box then shows whether the add-in is currently loaded (the Loaded/Unloaded box is checked), whether it's loaded automatically when the VB IDE loads (the Load on Startup box is checked), and whether it loads automatically when the VB IDE is launched using command-line arguments (the Command Line box is checked). Aside from reflecting the current state of the add-in, the user can also load the add-in, load the add-in automatically on startup, or load the add-in when VB is launched from the command line by checking the respective box.

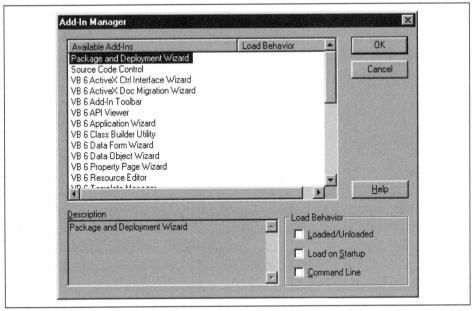

Figure 2-9. The VB6 Add-In Manager

As we have said, the VB5 Add-In Manager gets its list of add-ins from the *vbaddin.ini* file that resides in the Windows directory. VB6 doesn't require the use of the *vbaddin.ini* file. The necessary information is set in the Addin Class' dialog, which we discuss shortly, and stored in the registry.

For instance, the entry for our add-in shell in *vbaddin.ini* is:

```
AddInShell.Connect=1
```

The value 1 means that the add-in is activated as soon as VB starts (and so it's checked in the Add-In Manager). A value of 0 means that the add-in isn't activated automatically (and its checkbox isn't checked).

VB5 **Setting the vbaddin.ini reference**

There are several ways to set the necessary reference to an add-in in the *vbaddin.ini* file. We could:

- Provide the user with instructions on how to manually add the appropriate line to the *vbaddin.ini* file using a text editor

- Write a separate little VB utility that adds the appropriate line to *vbaddin.ini* automatically and instruct the user to run this utility

- Incorporate this step directly into the setup program for the add-in (the method for doing this depends upon how the setup program is created)

For our purposes, since we have access to the source code, a simple approach is to place code to do the registration in a separate procedure in the add-in itself. Thus, into a standard module (say, *basMain*) within the add-in, we would place the code shown in Example 2-1.

Example 2-1. Code to Register an Add-in in vbaddin.ini

```
Declare Function WritePrivateProfileString& Lib _
    "kernel32" Alias "WritePrivateProfileStringA" _
    (ByVal AppName$, ByVal KeyName$, _
    ByVal keydefault$, ByVal FileName$)


' -------------------------------------------------
' Execute ONCE from the Immediate window to add
' reference to add-in in the vbaddin.ini file.
'
' Don't forget to change the sProgID variable
' to the correct programmatic ID, i.e.
'
'        ProjectName.ConnectClassName
'
' -------------------------------------------------
Sub AddToINI()

Dim Resp As Long
Dim sProgID As String

sProgID = "AddInShell.Connect"    ' CHANGE THIS!

Resp = WritePrivateProfileString("Add-Ins32", _
  sProgID, "0", "vbaddin.ini")

If Resp = 0 Then
  MsgBox "Error adding add-in to vbaddin.ini."
Else
   MsgBox "Reference placed in vbaddin.ini."
End If

End Sub
```

Note the presence of the *WritePrivateProfile* function declaration, which should be placed in the Declarations section of the standard module. This function is part of the Windows API and is specifically designed to add new keys to an *INI* file. The third parameter of this function is set to "0" so that the add-in isn't checked in the Add-In Manager and, therefore, not loaded automatically when VB starts.

If we are distributing the source code of our add-in, then the user can also use this AddToINI procedure. Of course, we should inform the user that this procedure is included and needs to be run before the add-in is recognized by the Add-In Manager.

The Add-In Manager add-in name

As we discussed earlier, an add-in is identified, in the Add-In Manager and elsewhere, by its programmatic ID. Since this isn't a friendly name, VB allows us to replace this name in the Add-In Manager's list box (as you can see in Figure 2-8 and Figure 2-9).

VB5 In VB5, Microsoft has provided a rather unusual method for changing the name that the Add-In Manager uses to refer to an add-in. In particular, we invoke the Microsoft Object Browser (hit the F2 function key) and right-click on the Connect class object to bring up a context-sensitive menu. Choosing Properties from this menu produces the Member Options dialog box shown in Figure 2-10. From here we can set the Description for the Connect class. This description is what appears in the Add-In Manager.

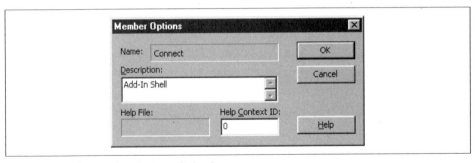

Figure 2-10. The Member Options dialog box

Note that we have deliberately chosen a description that places the add-in shell at the top of the Add-In Manager's list. This is very useful for a test add-in that is activated and deactivated often.

VB6 The process of setting an add-in's name is simpler under VB6; the AddIn Class designer's form is shown in Figure 2-11.

The General tab has a place to set the Add-in's display name, which is the name that appears in the Add-In Manager. The Add-in description also appears in the Add-In Manager. The Application list box should be set to Visual Basic. The Initial Load Behavior list box has four choices:

- Command Line/Startup
- Command Line
- Startup
- None

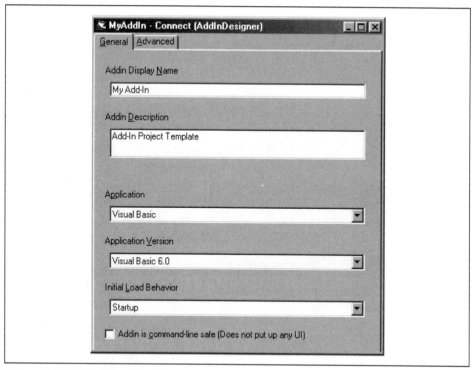

Figure 2-11. The AddIn Class' form

The reference to Command Line determines whether or not the add-in will start if VB is started from the command line. The reference to StartUp determines if the add-in starts automatically when VB is started.

The Add-In Toolbar

The Add-In Toolbar is an add-in whose sole purpose is to activate other add-ins.

As shown in Figure 2-12, this toolbar displays buttons for each installed add-in, as well as a button for installing or removing add-ins. Since add-ins are installed into the toolbar, the Add-In Toolbar doesn't use the *vbaddin.ini* file as the Add-In Manager does. (Nevertheless, if we're using VB5, we should still register an add-in in *vbaddin.ini* if we want it to be recognized by the Add-In Manager.)

Figure 2-12. The Add-In Toolbar

Clicking on the icon marked with a plus/minus sign brings up the dialog box shown in Figure 2-13, which isn't too dissimilar from the Add-In Manager's dialog box. (By the way, the list of add-ins that is shown in the Add-In Toolbar is kept in the system registry. The proper way to alter this list is to use the plus/minus button on the Add-In Toolbar itself.)

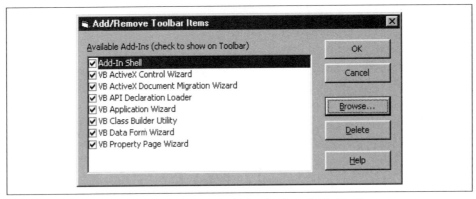

Figure 2-13. The Add/Remove Toolbar Items dialog for the Add-In Toolbar

The main advantage of the Add-In Toolbar over the Add-In Manager is that, since the toolbar is always visible, the Add-In Toolbar makes it easier to activate an add-in on the fly. On the other hand, the Add-In Toolbar doesn't provide for automatic add-in loading, as does the Add-In Manager.

We should also mention that the Add-In Toolbar is an in-process DLL whose filename is *aitool.dll;* it resides in the Wizards subdirectory of the Visual Basic directory. (You may need to pull it off the CD if it wasn't installed with VB.) Don't forget that the Add-In Toolbar, like all other add-ins, must be registered before it can be used.

Perhaps the most annoying feature of the Add-In Toolbar, which is certainly a nice utility, is that it isn't well documented. For instance, I haven't been able to find any information on how to set the button face for a new add-in, if indeed there is a way.

Note finally that the Add-In Toolbar is smart enough not to start a second instance of an add-in should the user click on that add-in's button a second time.

Connecting an Add-in

As we have discussed, add-ins don't create VBE objects, nor do they *ask* for a reference to an existing VBE object. Instead, they are *passed* a reference to this object by VB. In fact, the main design feature of an add-in, and the one that seems the most confusing, is a class module that exists specifically for the purpose of providing VB with a way to pass this reference to the add-in.

We saw in Chapter 1, *Introduction*, that, in VB5, every add-in must implement the four methods of the IDTExtensibility interface through a MultiUse public Connect class module. These methods are:

OnAdInsUpdate	OnDisconnection
OnConnection	OnStartupComplete

In VB6, the AddInInstance interface has seven methods:

Initialize	OnDisconnection
OnAdInsUpdate	OnStartupComplete
OnBeginShutdown	Terminate
OnConnection	

Now let's take a closer look at some of these methods. (The Initialize and Terminate methods are the first and last methods (events) to be fired, as is usual for any class module.)

The OnConnection Method

When we first attempt to activate an add-in, VB checks the registry for the information necessary to create an instance of the Connect class; that is, a Connect object. Once this object is created (and thus after the Initialize event has fired), VB can call the OnConnection method we have implemented for this object.

Under VB5, the syntax of the OnConnection method is:

```
Private Sub IDTExtensibility_OnConnection( _
    ByVal VBInst As Object, _
    ByVal ConnectMode As vbext_ConnectMode, _
    ByVal AddInInst As VBIDE.AddIn, _
    custom() As Variant)
```

Under VB6, the syntax is similar:

```
Private Sub AddinInstance_OnConnection( _
    ByVal Application As Object, _
    ByVal ConnectMode As AddInDesignerObjects.ext_ConnectMode, _
    ByVal AddInInst As Object, _
    custom() As Variant)
```

The first parameter, *VBInst* (in VB5) or *Application* (in VB6), is filled by VB with a reference to the VBE object for the current instance of the VB IDE. This is the main purpose of the OnConnection method. Thus, to us as add-in programmers, the OnConnection method acts precisely like an *event* that is fired by VB in response to the activation of the add-in.

The first thing we need to do in the OnConnection method is save the value of the parameter *VBInst* or *Application* in a module- or global-level variable, because once the OnConnection method terminates, this parameter is no longer valid. We need the VBE reference in order to manipulate the VB IDE object model, which is, after all, the whole point of the add-in. Thus, the minimal OnConnection implementation is simply (in VB5):

```
' Save the instance of VB
Set oVBE = VBInst
```

or (in VB6):

```
' Save the instance of VB
Set oVBE = Application
```

where *oVBE* is declared at the module level (preferably in a standard module) as:

```
Public oVBE As VBIDE.VBE
```

In VB5, The *ConnectMode* parameter can take on any of the values in the following enum:

```
Enum vbext_ConnectMode
    vbext_cm_AfterStartup = 0
    vbext_cm_Startup = 1
    vbext_cm_External = 2
End Enum
```

According to the documentation, in VB6, there is a fourth possible value:

```
vbext_cm_CommandLine
```

However, this constant doesn't appear in the *vb6ext.olb* object library.

In any case, these constants reflect the time or means by which the add-in is activated. In particular, if the add-in is activated automatically, the parameter is set (by VB) to **vbext_cm_Startup**. If the add-in is activated through the Add-In Manager after VB starts, the parameter is set to **vbext_cm_AfterStartup**. Finally, if the add-in is activated by an external source, such as another add-in (and this includes the Add-In Toolbar), the value of the parameter is set to **vbext_cm_External**.

Thus, we can use the value of the *ConnectMode* parameter to make our add-in behave differently based on how it's started. For instance, we may want to produce a message box of some sort if the add-in is activated after VB has started, but not otherwise.

As we will see, a portion of the VB IDE object model is devoted to add-ins themselves. The *AddInInst* parameter is set by VB to refer to the AddIn object that represents the current add-in. For instance, we can use this object to get the add-in's programmatic ID or description.

The *custom* parameter is, according to the Microsoft help file, "An array of variant expressions to hold user-defined data." Unfortunately, the documentation doesn't say how to use this parameter, or even why we would want to use it.

It's clear that the most important parameter to the OnConnection method is *VBInst* (in VB5) and *Application* (in VB6). In fact, it is the only parameter we must pay some attention to. Example 2-2 is a bare-bones OnConnection method written for VB5; for VB6 just change IDTExtensibility to AddinInstance and *VBInst* to *Application*.

Example 2-2. A Minimal OnConnection Event Handler

```
Private Sub IDTExtensibility_OnConnection( _
    ByVal VBInst As Object, _
    ByVal ConnectMode As vbext_ConnectMode, _
    ByVal AddInInst As VBIDE.AddIn, _
    custom() As Variant)

    On Error GoTo ERROR_CONNECT

    ' Save the instance of VB
    Set oVBE = VBInst

    ' Place code in following TEST AREA for testing
    ' objects of the VBIDE object model.
    '----------------------------------------


    '----------------------------------------

    ' Set breakpoint on following line for testing.
    Debug.Print "*** Started " & Now & " ***"

    Exit Sub

ERROR_CONNECT:

    MsgBox Err.Description

End Sub
```

Note that I have included some space for placing test code fragments, which I do from time to time (until I introduce a better way). We will refer to this area as the *test area* of the add-in.

Once execution reaches the test area in the OnConnection method, we have access to the VBIDE objects, so this is a reasonable place to do some fiddling. Also, we have included an additional line:

```
Debug.Print "*** Started " & Now & " ***"
```

which provides a convenient place for a breakpoint. It also serves to indicate in the Immediate window when the add-in was connected and to provide a useful demarcation point.

The BeginShutdown Method

The AddinInstance interface of VB6 includes an additional method not included in IDTExtensibility. The syntax is:

```
Sub BeginShutdown (Custom() As Variant)
```

This event is fired immediately before shutting down the VB IDE environment.

The OnDisconnection Method

The OnDisconnection method is fired by VB when we attempt to deactivate the add-in by unchecking it in the Add-In Manager or through code (using the add-in portion of the VB IDE object model).

In VB5, the syntax of the OnDisconnection method is:

```
Private Sub IDTExtensibility_OnDisconnection( _
    ByVal RemoveMode As vbext_DisconnectMode, _
    custom() As Variant)
```

where the *RemoveMode* parameter is filled by VB with one of the constants in the following enum:

```
Enum vbext_DisconnectMode
    vbext_dm_HostShutdown = 0
    vbext_dm_UserClosed = 1
End Enum
```

The value of *RemoveMode* is set to `vbext_dm_HostShutDown` if the add-in is being disconnected because VB is being closed, and it's set to `vbext_dm_User-Closed` if the add-in is being disconnected directly (through the Add-In Manager or by code). The *custom* parameter is the same as in the OnConnection method.

In VB6, the syntax is quite similar:

```
Private Sub AddinInstance_OnDisconnection( _
    ByVal RemoveMode As _
      AddInDesignerObjects.ext_DisconnectMode, _
    custom() As Variant)
```

and the parameters have the same meaning as in the VB5 case.

The OnDisconnection method doesn't need any specific code for the add-in to work (that is, beyond a comment so that the method is considered implemented). However, as we will see, most add-ins add items to the VB menu system or to a VB toolbar. The OnDisconnection method is the place to delete those items. (It would be very bad programming practice to leave orphaned menu or toolbar items in the VB IDE.)

Also, for debugging purposes, it's useful to include the following line in the OnDisconnection method:

```
Debug.Print "*** Ended " & Now & " ***"
```

In this way, all information sent to the Immediate window using `Debug.Print` is surrounded by two messages that include the time.

The OnStartupComplete Method

This method is fired by VB when the VB IDE finishes loading. Note that an add-in can be (and often is) connected after the VB IDE is loaded, so in this case, the method doesn't fire. However, the OnStartupComplete method does fire if the add-in is started along with the VB IDE, as is the case, for example, when the ProgID for the add-in is equal to 1 in the *vbaddin.ini* file.

Note that, if the add-in is loaded at startup, the OnConnection method fires before the OnStartupComplete method. Put another way, an add-in is connected *before* the VB IDE has finished loading. Thus, during add-in connection, the VB IDE isn't fully in place, so we can't yet fully manipulate the VB IDE object model. (For instance, the Windows collection of open VB windows can't be assumed to be fully populated until the VB IDE has finished loading.)

The OnAddInsUpdate Method

According to the VB5 documentation, the OnAddInsUpdate event "Occurs automatically when changes to the *Vbaddin.Ini* file are saved." However, this seems wrong. VB doesn't constantly poll the *vbaddin.ini* file to keep track of whether someone has opened it with a text editor and made changes. In general, we can safely ignore this poorly documented event. (The VB6 documentation says that this event is "Called when the add-ins collection changes.")

An Add-in Code Shell

Now we can put the pieces together to describe in brief the steps required to create an add-in code shell. You should make certain that your version includes all the following steps:

VB5

1. *Start an add-in project*

   Start a new ActiveX DLL project. Set the Startup option to (None) and give the project a name and description. For the purposes of our example, use the name "AddInShell" and description "Add-In Shell".

2. *Add a reference to the VB IDE object model*

Add a reference to the VB IDE object model in the References dialog box (under the Project menu), by selecting Microsoft Visual Basic 5.0 Extensibility. Also check the Microsoft Office Object Model reference.

3. *Create a standard module*

Create a standard module called *basMain*. Add the code shown below to the Declarations section:

```
Option Explicit

Public oVBE As VBIDE.VBE

Declare Function WritePrivateProfileString& Lib _
    "kernel32" Alias "WritePrivateProfileStringA" _
    (ByVal AppName$, ByVal KeyName$, _
    ByVal keydefault$, ByVal FileName$)
```

I should make a comment here about the *oVBE* declaration. Some developers choose to put this declaration in the Connect class module. While this works, it has two drawbacks. First, it makes the *oVBE* object accessible not only to the rest of the add-in project, but also to the rest of the world. This is bad form, since we don't want other applications to have access to this object. (It's really not even "our" object; it was given to us by VB in the OnConnection method.)

Second, we probably want to include supporting procedures that use the *oVBE* object. If we place this declaration in the class module, the object isn't accessible to the rest of the add-in project, so that all supporting procedures need to be placed in the Connect class as well. This bloats the public class with non-public code.

Next, create the *AddToINI* subroutine in *basMain*, as shown below:

```
' ------------------------------------------------
' Execute ONCE from the Immediate window to add
' reference in vbaddin.ini file.
'
' Don't forget to change the sProgID variable
' to the correct programmatic ID, i.e.
'
'         ProjectName.ConnectClassName
'
' ------------------------------------------------
Sub AddToINI()

Dim Resp As Long
Dim sProgID As String

sProgID = "AddInShell.Connect"

Resp = WritePrivateProfileString("Add-Ins32", _
```

```
       sProgID, "0", "vbaddin.ini")

   If Resp = 0 Then
     MsgBox "Error adding add-in to vbaddin.ini."
   Else
       MsgBox "Reference placed in vbaddin.ini."
   End If

   End Sub
```

4. *Add the Connect class module*

Add a class module to the add-in and name it Connect. (If the project already has a class module, just rename it Connect.) Set the Instancing property of the class to MultiUse (in the Properties window). Place the following in the Declarations section:

```
Option Explicit
Implements IDTExtensibility
```

Select IDTExtensibility in the Objects drop-down list box at the upper-left corner of the code window. (If this item isn't available, you probably forgot to set the reference to the extensibility object library.) Choose, in turn, each of the four methods in the Procedures drop-down list box. As the corresponding procedure code shells are created, add a single comment mark to each shell.

5. *Add the OnConnection and OnDisconnection methods*

For the OnConnection method, replace the comment mark with this code:

```
On Error GoTo ERROR_CONNECT

   ' Save the instance of VB
   Set oVBE = VBInst

   ' Place code in following TEST AREA for testing
   ' objects of the VBIDE object model.
   '----------------------------------------


   '----------------------------------------


   ' Set breakpoint on following line for testing.
   Debug.Print "*** Started " & Now & " ***"

   Exit Sub

ERROR_CONNECT:

   MsgBox Err.Description
```

In the OnDisconnection method, replace the comment mark with the line:

```
Debug.Print "*** Ended " & Now & " ***"
```

6. *Add the finishing touches*

Once the code is in place, there are two things that need to be done.

First, start the Object Browser (F2 function key) and select the library for your project from the upper-left drop-down list box. Then right-click on Connect in the classes list box. Choose Properties, and set the Description property to "Add-In Shell". As discussed, this defines the name for the add-in that is used by the Add-In Manager.

Second, make sure that the *sProgID* variable in the *AddToINI* procedure is set to the add-in's progID, and run the procedure once from the Immediate window to add the appropriate reference to *vbaddin.ini*.

VB6 1. *Start an add-in project*

Start a new ActiveX DLL project. Set the Startup option to (None) and give the project a name and description. For the purposes of our example, use the name "AddInShell" and description "Add-In Shell".

2. *Add a reference to the VB IDE object model*

Add a reference to the VB IDE object model in the References dialog box (under the Project menu) by selecting Microsoft Visual Basic 6.0 Extensibility. Also check the Microsoft Office Object Model reference.

3. *Create a standard module*

Create a standard module called *basMain*. Add the code shown below to the Declarations section:

```
Option Explicit

Public oVBE As VBIDE.VBE
```

I should make a comment here about the *oVBE* declaration. Some developers choose to put this declaration in the Connect class module. While this works, it has two drawbacks. First, it makes the *oVBE* object accessible not only to the rest of the add-in project, but also to the rest of the world. This is bad form, since we don't want other applications to have access to this object. (It's really not even "our" object; it was given to us by VB in the OnConnection method.)

Second, we probably want to include supporting procedures that use the *oVBE* object. If we place this declaration in the class module, the object isn't accessible to the rest of the add-in project, so all supporting procedures need to be placed in the Connect class as well. This bloats the public class with nonpublic code.

4. *Add the Connect class module*

Add an Addin Class designer to the add-in project. First, select the Components dialog on the Project menu. The dialog is shown earlier in Figure 2-3. On the Designers tab, check the Addin Class designer and hit the OK button. (Incidentally, the help documentation incorrectly refers to this entry as the AddInDesigner object.)

Next, choose the Add Addin Class menu item from the Projects menu. (Again, the help documentation incorrectly refers to this menu item as AddInDesigner.) This places a new designer in the project. Set the designer's name to Connect and its Public property to True. This designer *implicitly* adds the code:

```
Implements AddInInstance
```

to the project. (Thus, we don't need to add this line.) However, according to the documentation, we do need to implement the methods of the AddInInstance interface.

Select AddinInstance in the Objects drop-down list box at the upper-left corner of the code window. (If this item isn't available, then you probably forgot to set the reference to the extensibility object library.) Choose, in turn, each of the methods in the Procedures drop-down list box. As the corresponding procedure code shells are created, add a single comment mark to each shell. (It isn't entirely clear that all these methods really need to be implemented. I have been able to create add-ins that don't implement all of the methods, but I certainly would not release such an add-in for distribution. Why take the chance?)

5. *Add the OnConnection and OnDisconnection methods*

For the OnConnection method, replace the comment mark with this code:

```
On Error GoTo ERROR_CONNECT

    ' Save the instance of VB
    Set oVBE = Application

    ' Place code in following TEST AREA for testing
    ' objects of the VBIDE object model.
    '----------------------------------------


    '----------------------------------------


    ' Set breakpoint on following line for testing.
    Debug.Print "*** Started " & Now & " ***"

    Exit Sub

ERROR_CONNECT:

    MsgBox Err.Description
```

In the OnDisconnection method, replace the comment mark with the line:

```
Debug.Print "*** Ended " & Now & " ***"
```

6. *Add the finishing touches*

Display the Connect designer's form to access the designer's dialog, as in Figure 2-14, and fill in the dialog as shown.

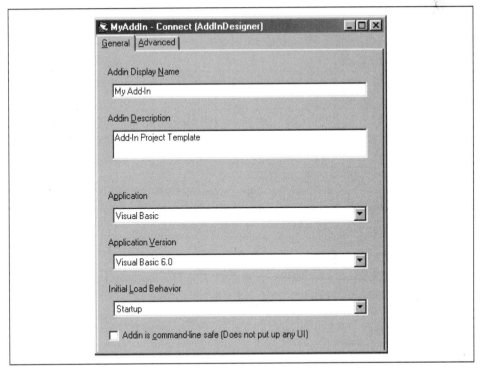

Figure 2-14. The Addin Class Designer dialog

Try It Out

To test the add-in code shell, let's place some code in the OnConnection method and activate the add-in. First, place the following line of code in the test area of the OnConnection method:

```
' Place code here for testing objects of
' the VBIDE object model.
'----------------------------------------
MsgBox "Project name: " & oVBE.VBProjects(1).Name
'----------------------------------------
```

Now save the project and start it. Open another copy of VB and choose standard EXE. We will refer to this project or any project used to test our add-in as the *client project* from now on (since it's the client of the add-in). Start the client project's Add-In Manager and select the Add-In Shell checkbox (in VB5) or check the Loaded/Unloaded box (in VB6). Dismiss the Add-In Manager to activate the add-in.

Depending on various circumstances, you may or may not see a message box. If not, then switching to the add-in project should bring the message box shown in Figure 2-15 to the foreground.

Figure 2-15. Testing the add-in

The problem is that the add-in is being run from another instance of VB and hence in a different process than the client. In other words, even though we are creating an in-process DLL add-in, when it's being run from the VB IDE, it acts as an out-of-process add-in. Accordingly, the message box may be buried under the windows of the current instance of VB—the one that activated the add-in.

The good news is that this problem goes away when the add-in is actually running on its own as a DLL, for then it lies in the same process as the client. To illustrate, do the following:

1. Uncheck the add-in from the Add-In Manager.

2. Return to the add-in shell project and stop the project.

3. Make an ActiveX DLL version of the add-in but don't start the add-in project itself.

4. Return to the client project and select the add-in in the Add-In Manager. This time you should see the message box as soon as you dismiss the Add-In Manager. You have just completed your first add-in!

You may wonder what would happen if we ran the add-in project from the VB IDE after having created an executable (DLL). Fortunately, VB is smart enough to use the version of the add-in that is running in the VB IDE, ignoring the executable. Thus, we don't need to delete the DLL before doing further testing of the add-in project from the VB IDE.

Before proceeding further, you should remove or comment out the line:

```
MsgBox "Project name: " & oVBE.VBProjects(1).Name
```

We should also note that there are some things that can't be done from an out-of-process add-in, and thus from a DLL that is being run from the VB IDE. For instance, **SendKeys** statements don't work, because they send the keystrokes to the add-in rather than to its client. Thus, there will be times when we need to recompile our add-in as a DLL and use that DLL for testing. Of course, this may require some additional "tricks" to get information from the DLL. In particular, since we can't send information to the Immediate window, we need alternatives, such as perhaps writing to a disk file, or using beep codes, which we cover in Chapter 5, *Debugging Add-ins*.

A VB add-in can include form modules and display both modal and nonmodal forms just like any other program. In fact, you can try it out by adding a form module to the add-in shell and invoking that form's Show method in the test area of our add-in shell.

There is, however, one thing to keep in mind about nonmodal forms. If the user causes a nonmodal form in an add-in to be displayed and then deactivates the add-in without first unloading the form, the form isn't automatically unloaded, and the user ends up with an orphaned form. Thus, it's important to place an `Unload` statement in the OnDisconnection method. Indeed, nonmodal forms can easily get lost in the pile of windows that is usually present during VB programming, so it's better to use modal forms if at all possible.

We now know how to construct a basic add-in shell. There is one more piece of the add-in puzzle that needs to be discussed before we can study the VB IDE object model. Namely, most add-ins require that we add menu items or toolbar buttons to the VB IDE, so that the user can invoke the features of the add-in. Thus, we need to take a look at the process of altering VB's menus and toolbars. As it happens, this is done by manipulating another object model, so we next turn to a discussion of object models in general.

In this chapter:
- *Collection Objects*
- *Object Model Hierarchies*
- *Object Model Syntax*
- *Object Variables*

3

Object Models

Our plan in this chapter is to discuss object models in general, although our examples will come from the VB IDE object model. We will not go into great detail, but the material is important in understanding the basics of object models, since writing useful add-ins requires knowledge of both the VB IDE object model and the CommandBars portion of the Office object model.

If you are familiar with object models, you may need only to skim this chapter quickly.

Collection Objects

In programming with the VB IDE object model (or indeed any object model), it's common to have a great many objects "alive" at the same time. To manage these objects, the designers of an object model generally include special types of objects called *collection objects.*

As the name implies, collection objects represent collections of objects—generally objects of a single type. For instance, the VB IDE object model has a collection object called VBComponents that represents all of the components (forms, modules, and classes) in a project.

Collection objects are generally just called *collections,* but it's very important to remember that a collection is just a special type of object. As we will see, the properties and methods of a Collection object are specifically designed to manage the collection.

We can generally spot a collection object by the fact that its name is the plural of the name of the objects contained within the collection. For instance, the VBComponents collection contains VBComponent objects. However, this isn't a hard and fast rule. For instance, the SelectedVBControls collection contains VBControl objects, not SelectedVBControl objects (which don't even exist).

Collections are extremely common in the VB IDE object model. In fact, of the approximately 50 objects in the model, 19 of them are collection objects.

I emphasize the fact that a collection is just a special type of object. Indeed, the properties and methods of a Collection object are specifically designed to manage the collection. Accordingly, the *basic* requirements for a collection object are:

- A property called Count that returns the number of objects in the collection. This is a read-only property; that is, it can't be set by the programmer and is automatically updated by VB itself.

- A method called Add (or something similar, such as AddNew or AddItem or even Open) that allows the programmer to add a new object to the collection.

- A method called Delete or Remove or Close (or something similar) that allows the programmer to remove an object from the collection.

- A method called Item that permits the programmer to access any particular object in the collection. The item is usually identified either by name or by an index number.

Note that these basic requirements aren't set in stone. Some collection objects may not implement all of these members and many implement additional members.

Let's elaborate a bit on the Item method. Consider the VBProjects collection object, which contains all the open projects in the VB IDE. (I go into the details of this in Chapter 8, *Project-Related Objects*.) The second project is thus denoted by:

```
VBProjects(2)
```

Moreover, a project whose name is Aproject can be identified by:

```
VBProjects("Aproject")
```

where the project's name is enclosed in quotation marks.

We should take a moment to discuss the base of a collection. Most collections, such as the VBProjects collection, are *one-based*, which means that the first element of the collection has index 1. Some collections in some Microsoft object models, particularly older models, are *zero-based*, which means that the first element of the collection has index 0. (For instance, the UserForms collection, which appears in several Microsoft object models, but not in the extensibility model, is zero-based.) Unfortunately, the base of a collection is seldom clearly documented, and so it's generally up to us to test the base using a bit of code. For instance, if the code:

```
MsgBox VBProjects(0).Name
```

generates a runtime "Subscript out of range" error (in the case that there are some existing VBProjects), then we know that the collection is one-based.

Object Model Hierarchies

The fact that one object's properties and methods can return another object, thus creating the concept of *child objects*, is of paramount importance, for it adds a useful structure to the object model.

By looking at the literature, it seems that there is no total agreement on when one object is considered a child of another object. However, it can be said that if object A has a property or method that returns object B, object B is a child of object A, and object A is a parent of object B.

Incidentally, it's important not to take the parent-child analogy too literally. For instance, the object hierarchy is full of circular parent-child relationships. In fact, an object can be a child of itself. For instance, the Window object has a Linked-WindowFrame property that returns a Window object.

The object hierarchy of an object model is often pictured in a tree-like structure. A portion of the VB IDE object model is shown in Figure 3-1.

Figure 3-1 is a screen shot of the Enhanced Object Browser, written by me, a coupon for which is included at the back of this book. The question marks in front of an object indicate that help is available from Microsoft's help files (usually). The small basket means that the object is a collection. Noncollection objects are indicated by small ovals. The plus sign following the object means that the object has children that aren't currently showing.

Object Model Syntax

Let's now discuss the basic syntax used when programming with an object model.

The general syntax for referring to an object's properties and methods is simple. If *objVar* is an object variable that refers to a particular object, and **AProperty** is a property of this object, we can access this property (for reading or for changing) using the syntax:

```
objVar.AProperty(any required parameters)
```

For instance, the following code sets the Name property of the first open project in the current IDE:

```
oVBE.VBProjects(1).Name = "ThisProject"
```

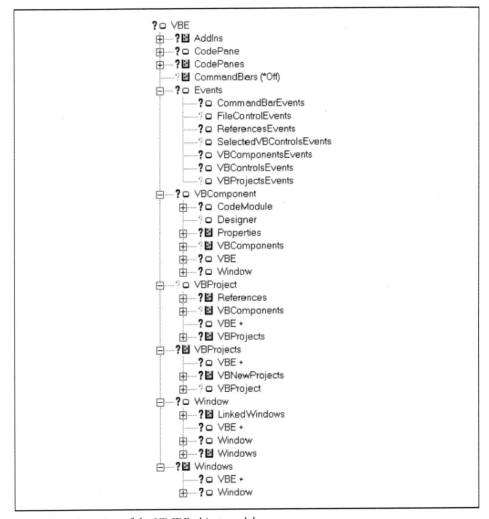

Figure 3-1. A portion of the VB IDE object model

Alternately, we can use an object variable as follows:

```
Dim proj As VBProject
Set proj = oVBE.VBProjects(1)
proj.Name = "ThisProject"
```

If AMethod is a method for this object, we can invoke that method with the syntax:

```
objVar.AMethod(any required parameters)
```

For instance, continuing the previous code, we can apply the MakeCompiledFile method to the project referred to by *proj* as follows:

```
proj.MakeCompiledFile
```

This method compiles the project into an executable (EXE, DLL, or whatever).

Object Variables

An *object variable* is a variable whose type is an object type. A generic object variable is declared as follows:

```
Dim proj As Object
```

A specific object variable is declared as a specific object type, as in:

```
Dim proj As VBProject
```

As we have said, the VB IDE object model has about 50 objects, and we can declare object variables of each of these types.

The Set Statement

Declaring object variables is done in the same way as declaring nonobject variables. On the other hand, assigning a value to an object variable must be done using the **Set** keyword. For example, the following line assigns the currently active VB project to the variable *proj*:

```
Set proj = oVBE.ActiveVBProject
```

The Is Operator

The act of comparing two variables also differs more for object variables than for nonobject variables. In particular, it requires use of the **Is** operator, as in:

```
If proj1 Is proj2 then . . .
```

Using Object Variables

Object variables are actually more important than might seem at first, because they can make programs run much more quickly. For instance, to execute each of the lines in the following code:

```
oVBE.Windows(1).Top = 100
oVBE.Windows(1).Left = 100
oVBE.Windows(1).Height = 1000
oVBE.Windows(1).Width = 1000
```

VB needs to resolve the references to the Windows object; that is, it needs to navigate the VB IDE object model. This takes time.

However, if we write:

```
Dim w as VBIDE.Window
Set w = oVBE.Windows(1)
```

```
w.Top = 100
w.Left = 100
w.Height = 1000
w.Width = 1000
```

then VB only needs to resolve the reference to the Window object once.

The With Statement

VB supplies the `With` statement to use with code such as the code above. In particular, we could write:

```
Dim w as VBIDE.Window
Set w = oVBE.Windows(1)
With w
    .Top = 100
    .Left = 100
    .Height = 1000
    .Width = 1000
End With
```

which is both more readable than the previous code and executes more rapidly (although in this small example, the difference would not be noticeable). The general syntax of the `With` statement is:

```
With object
    ' statements go here
End With
```

where the statements generally refer to the object, but don't require qualification using the object's name.

An Object Variable Is a Pointer

There are some very important differences between object variables and nonobject variables. A nonobject variable can be thought of as a name for a location in the computer's memory that holds the data referred to by the variable. For instance, in the code:

```
Dim iVar As Integer
iVar = 123
```

the variable *iVar* is a four-byte memory location that holds the integer value 123. This can be pictured as in Figure 3-2. (Actually, the four-byte memory location holds the value 123 in binary format, but that isn't relevant to our discussion.)

Now, if we were to further write:

```
Dim iVar2 As Integer
iVar2 = iVar
iVar2 = 567
```

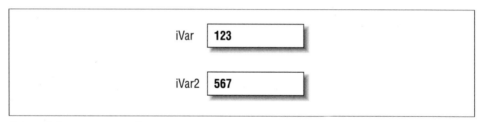

Figure 3-2. Integers stored in memory

we wouldn't expect the last line of code to have any effect upon the value of the variable *iVar*, which should still be 123. This is because *iVar* and *iVar2* represent different areas of memory, as pictured in Figure 3-2.

However, an object variable isn't the name of a memory location that holds the object. Rather, an object variable is the name of a memory location that holds the *address of* the memory location that holds the object, as shown in Figure 3-3. Put another way, the object variable holds a *reference to*, or *points to*, the object. For this reason, it's an example of a pointer variable, or simply a pointer. In Figure 3-3, for example, the object variable *proj1* points to an object of type VBProject.

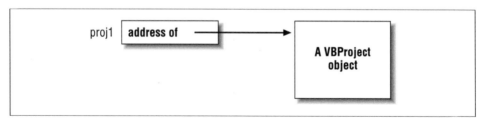

Figure 3-3. An object variable in memory

The code that might go with Figure 3-3, where *proj1* refers to the first open project in the current VB IDE, is:

```
Dim proj1 as VBProject
Set proj1 = oVBE.VBProjects(1)
```

One of the consequences of the fact that object variables are pointers is that more than one object variable can point to (or refer to) the same object, as in:

```
Dim proj1, proj2 as VBProject
Set proj1 = oVBE.VBProjects(1)
Set proj2 = proj1
```

This code creates the situation pictured in Figure 3-4. I emphasize that while *proj1* and *proj2* are different object variables, they hold the same value and so point to the same object. Thus, we can change the project using either of these object variables.

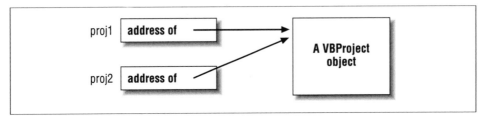

Figure 3-4. Two object variables referencing the same object

It's important when programming with objects to keep careful track of all object variables and what they are referencing. Furthermore, it's generally not a good idea to have more than one object variable pointing to the same object (as in Figure 3-4) unless there is a compelling reason to do so, for it's easy to change the object using one object variable (say *proj1*) and then later use the other variable (*proj2*), thinking it refers to the unchanged object.

Freeing an Object Variable: The Nothing Keyword

To free an object variable so that it no longer points to anything, we use the Nothing keyword, as in:

```
Set proj = Nothing
```

It's good programming practice to free object variables (by setting them to Nothing) when they are no longer needed, since this can save resources. (An object variable is set to Nothing automatically when its lifetime expires.)

Note that once an object no longer has any references to it, the object is automatically destroyed by VB, thus freeing up its resources (memory). However, *all* references to the object must be freed before the object is destroyed. This is another reason not to point more than one object variable at the same object if possible.

To test whether or not an object variable has been set to Nothing, we write:

```
If proj1 Is Nothing Then . . .
```

Default Members

Many (but not all) VBIDE objects have a *default member* (property or method) that is invoked when a property or method is expected but one isn't specified. For instance, the default member for the VBProject object is the Name property. Hence, the code:

```
Dim proj As VBProject
Set proj = oVBE.VBProjects(1)
proj = "ThisProject"
```

sets the first VB project's name to ThisProject, since VB applies the default property in the last line, effectively replacing it with:

```
proj.Name = "ThisProject"
```

Note the difference between:

```
proj2 = proj1
```

and:

```
Set proj2 = proj1
```

In the latter case, the variable *proj2* is set to refer to the VB project pointed to by *proj1*. In the former case, *proj2* and *proj1* still point to their original projects. Only the name in project *proj2* is changed.

Of course, we are free to use default members whenever we wish, and Microsoft uses them often in their help documentation. However, default members tend to make code less readable, and for this reason, they are generally avoided in this book.

One notable exception is for a collection object. It's usually the case that the default member of a collection object is the Item method. Hence, for instance, we can refer to the second project in the current IDE by:

```
oVBE.VBProjects(2)
```

rather than the more clumsy:

```
oVBE.VBProjects.Item(2)
```

Since this use of the default member isn't likely to cause any confusion, we will use it.

4

Menus and Toolbars

Most add-ins require that menu items or toolbar buttons be added to the VB IDE so that the user can invoke its features. In this chapter, we discuss methods for programmatically controlling menus and toolbars.

Menus and Toolbars: An Overview

The VB menu and toolbar system involves only a small number of objects, but they cross two object models. Let's briefly outline these objects. We will, of course, elaborate on this outline in the rest of the chapter. Note that menus and toolbars are both types of *command bars*.

The VBE object (see Figure 4-1) has an Events child object, which in turn has a CommandBarEvents child object. This object receives the Click event of a menu item or toolbar button. As we will see, this gives us the ability to place event code in a Click event for a menu or toolbar item.

In addition, the VBE object has a property named CommandBars that provides access to the CommandBars collection, which is part of the Office object model and is used by the applications in the Office application suite. Figure 4-2 shows that portion of the Office object model that relates to menus and toolbars. Note that this object model is quite small, containing only two objects and their corresponding collections:

- CommandBar objects and CommandBars collections

- CommandBarControl objects and CommandBarControls collections

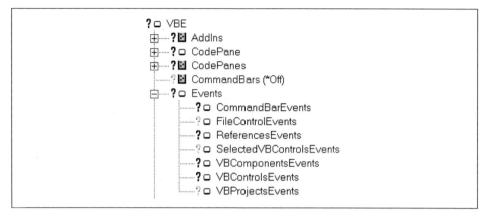

Figure 4-1. The CommandBarEvents object

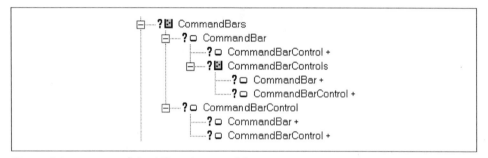

Figure 4-2. A portion of the Office object model

Menu Terminology

To help set the terminology, Figure 4-3 shows the components of a typical menu. (This figure is taken from a Microsoft Word menu, but the terms are the same for VB menus.)

The CommandBar Object

Toolbars, menu bars, menus, submenus, and shortcut menus are all CommandBar objects. (A shortcut menu is a menu that pops up at various locations on the screen in response to a right mouse click.)

It's important to note, however, that Office VBA doesn't treat each of these CommandBar objects in the same way. For instance, the Count property of the CommandBars collection counts only the top-level items: menu bars, toolbars, and shortcut menus. It doesn't count menus or submenus. Also, the Add method of the CommandBars collection can create toolbars or menu bars, but not menus or submenus.

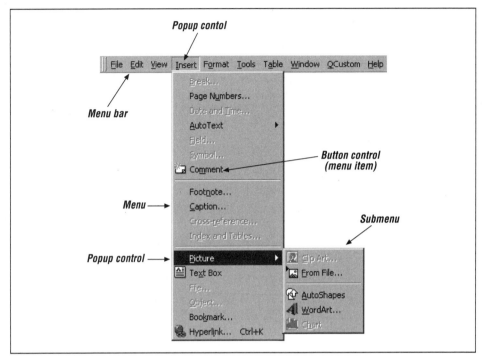

Figure 4-3. The menu structure

The CommandBar object has a Type property that can assume one of the constants in the following enum:

```
Enum MsoBarType
    msoBarTypeNormal = 0    ' toolbar
    msoBarTypeMenuBar = 1   ' menu bar
    msoBarTypePopup = 2     ' menu, submenu or shortcut menu
End Enum
```

Command Bar Controls

The items appearing on a toolbar, menu bar, menu, or submenu are actually controls, called *command bar controls*; that is, they are CommandBarControl objects. As we will see, there are various types of command bar controls, falling into two broad categories:

- Custom command bar controls (including custom text boxes, drop-down list boxes, and combo boxes)

- Built-in command bar controls

Note that command bar controls aren't the same as the controls we place on forms; they are designed specifically for toolbars and menus.

There are two special types of custom command bar controls that aren't typical of other types of controls:

Popup controls

A command bar control of type `msoControlPopup` is a control whose sole purpose is to pop up a menu (when the control is on a menu bar) or a submenu (when the control is on a menu). These controls are naturally referred to as *popup controls* (see Figure 4-3). Popup controls that are located on a menu bar take on the appearance of a recessed button when the mouse pointer is over the control. Popup controls on a menu or submenu have a small arrow on the far right to identify them.

Thus, the term "popup" is unfortunately used in two different ways. A *popup control* is a command bar control of type `msoControlPopup` and is used to pop up a menu or submenu. A *popup command bar* is a command bar of type `msoBarTypePopup` and is either a menu, submenu, or shortcut menu. (In other words, a popup control causes a popup command bar to pop up!)

Button controls

A command bar control of type `msoControlButton` is called a *button control*. When a button control is activated (using an accelerator key or mouse click), a Click event occurs. It's the purpose of the CommandBarEvents object of the VB IDE object model to "hook" into this event.

Adding a menu

We might at first think that adding a new menu to a menu bar is done using the Add method of the CommandBars collection, specifying the name of the parent menu and the location of the new menu on the parent. After all, a menu is a CommandBar object, and this procedure would be consistent with other cases of adding objects to a collection.

However, this isn't how it's done. Instead, as we will see, a new menu (or submenu) is created by adding a command bar control of type `msoControlPopup` to the CommandBarControls collection of the parent menu (and specifying the new control's position on the parent). Actually, this represents a savings of effort on our behalf. For, as we have remarked, a menu or submenu requires a popup control for activation. Thus, Microsoft makes the task of creating menus and submenus easier by automatically creating the corresponding (empty) menu or submenu in response to our creation of a popup control. (We will see an example of this in the later section "Example: Creating a Menu," so don't worry too much if this isn't perfectly clear yet.)

Menus and Toolbars: The Object Model

Now that we have discussed the terminology used in describing menus, we can examine how an application's menus and toolbars are programmatically controlled through the Office and VBE object models.

The CommandBars Collection

The topmost object in the Office object model that relates to menus and toolbars is the CommandBars collection, which contains all the application's CommandBar objects.

To access the CommandBars collection for the VB IDE, we use the CommandBars property of the VBE object. Before we can manipulate the Office object model, a reference must be set to the Microsoft Office Object Library in the References dialog.

Now, in the test area of the OnConnection method (for the add-in shell project), add the following code:

```
Dim sType As String
Dim cbar As Office.CommandBar

Debug.Print "Count: " & oVBE.CommandBars.Count

Debug.Print "NAME,TYPE,VISIBLE"

For Each cbar In oVBE.CommandBars

  Select Case cbar.Type
  Case msoBarTypeNormal        ' a toolbar
    sType = "Normal"
  Case msoBarTypeMenuBar      ' a menu bar
    sType = "Menu bar"
  Case msoBarTypePopup        ' a shortcut menu
    sType = "Popup"
    ' Next line is for later use
    ' If cbar.Name = "Document" Then _
         cbar.ShowPopup
  End Select

  Debug.Print cbar.Name & "," & sType _
    & "," & cbar.Visible

Next
```

The purpose of this code is to print a list of all of the CommandBar objects currently available in the client VB IDE to the Immediate window. Example 4-1 shows the printout for my system.

Example 4-1. A Listing of Available CommandBar Objects

```
Count: 29
NAME,TYPE,VISIBLE
Menu Bar,Menu bar,True
Standard,Normal,False
Edit,Normal,False
Debug,Normal,False
Form Editor,Normal,False
Document,Popup,False
Project Window Insert,Popup,False
Toggle,Popup,False
Code Window,Popup,False
Code Window (Break),Popup,False
Watch Window,Popup,False
Immediate Window,Popup,False
Locals Window,Popup,False
Forms,Popup,False
Controls,Popup,False
Project Window,Popup,False
Project Window (Break),Popup,False
Form Layout Window,Popup,False
Object Browser,Popup,False
Toolbox,Popup,False
Toolbox Group,Popup,False
Property Browser,Popup,False
Color Palette,Popup,False
Project Window Project,Popup,False
Project Window Form Folder,Popup,False
Project Window Module/Class Folder,Popup,False
Project Window Related Documents Folder,Popup,False
Docked Window,Popup,False
Custom 1,Normal,False
```

As mentioned earlier, even though menu bars, menus, submenus, shortcut menus and toolbars are all CommandBar objects, Office VBA doesn't treat each of these CommandBar objects in the same way. For instance, the Count property of the CommandBars collection counts only menu bars, toolbars, and shortcut menus. It doesn't count menus or submenus.

Also, by Microsoft's design, the **For Each** loop in the previous code picks up only toolbars, menu bars, and shortcut menus. Finally, the Add method of the CommandBars collection can create toolbars or menu bars, but not menus or submenus. (The latter are created using the Add method of the CommandBarControls collection.)

Just for fun, uncomment out the line that begins **If cbar.Name =** and then run the add-in again. When you activate the add-in from the client, do so with the keyboard, leaving the mouse pointer in the middle of the screen. You should see the Document shortcut menu at the cursor location, just as though the right mouse button was clicked.

Creating a new menu bar or toolbar

To create a new menu bar, use the Add method of the CommandBars collection. The syntax for the Add method is:

```
CommandBarsObject.Add(Name, Position, MenuBar, _
    Temporary)
```

The optional *Name* parameter is the name of the new command bar. If this argument is omitted, a default name (such as "Custom 1") is assigned to the command bar. The optional *Position* parameter gives the position of the new command bar. This can be set to **msoBarLeft**, **msoBarTop**, **msoBarRight**, **msoBarBottom**, **msoBarFloating** (for a floating command bar), or **msoBarPopup** (for a shortcut menu).

The optional Boolean *MenuBar* parameter is set to **True** for a menu bar and **False** for a toolbar. The default value is **False**, so if the argument is omitted, a toolbar is created. Note that if we create a new menu bar and make it visible, it replaces the existing VB menu bar. (If this happens, you can still exit VB using Alt+F4.)

Setting the optional *Temporary* parameter to **True** makes the new command bar temporary. Temporary command bars are deleted when VB is closed. The default value is **False**.

To illustrate, the following code creates a new permanent floating toolbar called TestCB and makes it visible:

```
Dim cbar As Office.CommandBar

Set cbar = oVBE.CommandBars.Add("TestCB", _
    msoBarFloating, False, True)

cbar.Visible = True
```

You can test this code by placing it in the test area of the OnConnection method, as usual. Note that it's necessary to set the Visible property of the command bar to **True**, since the default value is **False**.

It's important to note that, if a CommandBar object by the name TestCB already exists, the previous code produces a runtime illegal procedure error. Thus, we really should test for the existence of a CommandBar object before using the Add method, as in the following code:

```
Dim cbar As Office.CommandBar
Dim bExists As Boolean
bExists = False
For Each cbar In oVBE.CommandBars
    If cbar.Name = "TestCB" Then bExists = True
Next
```

```
If Not bExists Then
    Set cbar = oVBE.CommandBars.Add("TestCB", _
        msoBarFloating, False, True)
    cbar.Visible = True
End If
```

Command Bar Controls

Initially, one of the most confusing aspects of the Office/VB menu system is that the items that appear on a menu bar are not menus, or even names of menus. Rather, they are controls of type CommandBarControl. Command bar controls can be added to a menu bar, toolbar, menu, submenu, or shortcut menu.

Every command bar control is an object of type CommandBarControl and so it belongs to the CommandBarControls collection. (We aren't saying that the Type property of a CommandBarControl is CommandBarControl.) In addition, every command bar control is an object of one of the following three object types:

- CommandBarButton

- CommandBarComboBox

- CommandBarPopup

This dual identity of CommandBarControl objects allows the various types of command bar controls to possess on the one hand, a common set of properties and methods (those of the CommandBarControl object), and on the other hand, an additional set of properties and methods that reflects the diversity of these controls. This makes sense, since for instance text boxes are quite different from popup controls. Moreover, as we will see, CommandBarPopup objects need a special property (called Controls) that provides access to the associated menu's controls. (The other types of CommandBarControl objects don't need, and don't have, this property.)

The Type property of a CommandBarControl helps to identify the data type of the control. The Type property can assume any of the values in the following enum:

```
Enum MsoControlType
    msoControlCustom = 0
    msoControlButton = 1              ' CommandBarButton
    msoControlEdit = 2                ' CommandBarComboBox
    msoControlDropdown = 3            ' CommandBarComboBox
    msoControlComboBox = 4            ' CommandBarComboBox
    msoControlButtonDropdown = 5      ' CommandBarComboBox
    msoControlSplitDropdown = 6       ' CommandBarComboBox
    msoControlOCXDropdown = 7         ' CommandBarComboBox
    msoControlGenericDropdown = 8
    msoControlGraphicDropdown = 9     ' CommandBarComboBox
    msoControlPopup = 10              ' CommandBarPopup
    msoControlGraphicPopup = 11       ' CommandBarPopup
```

```
        msoControlButtonPopup = 12            ' CommandBarPopup
        msoControlSplitButtonPopup = 13       ' CommandBarPopup
        msoControlSplitButtonMRUPopup = 14    ' CommandBarPopup
        msoControlLabel = 15
        msoControlExpandingGrid = 16
        msoControlSplitExpandingGrid = 17
        msoControlGrid = 18
        msoControlGauge = 19
        msoControlGraphicCombo = 20           ' CommandBarComboBox
    End Enum
```

The comments that follow some of the constants in this enum indicate the data type of the control. This information comes from the Microsoft help files. The missing comments mean that either some command bar controls don't belong to one of the three data types in question or that the help file hasn't kept up with later additions to the enum.

Creating a new command bar control

To create and add a command bar control to a command bar, use the Add method of the CommandBarControls collection. This method returns a CommandBarButton, CommandBarComboBox, or CommandBarPopup object, depending on the value of the *Type* parameter (see below). The syntax is

```
    CommandBarControlsObject.Add(Type, Id, Parameter, _
        Before, Temporary)
```

Type is the type of control to be added to the specified command bar. Table 4-1 shows the possible values for this parameter, along with the corresponding control and the return type of the Add method.

Table 4-1. msoControlType Values for the Type Parameter

Type Parameter (Value)	Control	Returned Object
msoControlButton (1)	Button	CommandBarButton
msoControlEdit (2)	Text box	CommandBarComboBox
msoControlDropdown (3)	List box	CommandBarComboBox
soControlComboBox (4)	Combo box	CommandBarComboBox
msoControlPopup (10)	Popup	CommandBarPopup

The optional *Before* parameter is a number that indicates the position of the new control on the command bar. The new control is inserted before the control that is at this position. If this argument is omitted, the control is added at the end of the command bar.

To add a so-called custom control of one of the types listed in Table 4-1, set the *Id* parameter to 1 or leave it out. To add a built-in control, we would set the *Id* parameter to the ID number of the control (and leave out the *Type* argument). We will discuss built-in control IDs in the next section.

As with command bars, we can set the optional *Temporary* parameter to **True** to make the new command bar control temporary. It will then be deleted when VB is closed.

It's very important to note that a CommandBar object doesn't have a Command-BarControls property, as might be expected. In order to return a CommandBar-Controls object, we must use the Controls property, as in:

```
CommandBars("Menu bar").Controls
```

It's equally important to note that, among all of the types of CommandBarControls, one and only one type has a Controls property. In particular, a Command-BarControl of type CommandBarPopup has a Controls property, which provides access to the CommandBarControls collection associated with the corresponding menu for the popup control. As we will see in later examples, the Controls property thus provides the means by which we can add controls to the menu.

Built-in command bar control IDs

As seen in the toolbar example below, it's possible to place built-in command bar controls on toolbars (or menus). This is done by setting the *Id* parameter of the Add method of the CommandBarControls collection to the ID of the built-in command bar control.

We must now address the issue of how to determine the IDs for the built-in controls. One approach to finding the ID of a particular control is to use the FindControl method to get a reference to the control. Once this is done, we can examine the control's ID property. The syntax for FindControl is:

```
expression.FindControl(Type, Id, Tag, Visible, Recursive)
```

where *expression* is either a CommandBar or CommandBars object. The other parameters are optional. The method returns the *first* CommandBarControl object that fits the criteria specified by the parameters. Briefly, the parameters are:

Type
    One of the **MsoControlType** constants in the enum given above

Id
    The ID of the control

Tag
    The tag value of the control

Visible
    Set to **True** to include only visible command bar controls in the search

Recursive

True to include the command bar and all of its popup sub-toolbars in the search

While the FindControl method can be quite useful, the problem in this situation is that the method requires another way to identify the control, such as through its Tag property. Thus, the FindControl method is most useful in finding a custom control that we have created and assigned a Tag value.

An alternative approach to getting built-in control IDs is to create a one-time list for future reference. The following code, which can be placed in the test area, creates a text file and fills it with a list of all built-in control names and IDs. The code creates a temporary toolbar, adds a built-in control for each possible control ID using a simple For loop, and then examines each of these controls. This is a rather ad hoc approach, but this seems to be the only approach available.

```
Dim fr As Integer
Dim cbar As Office.CommandBar
Dim ctl As CommandBarControl
Dim i As Integer
Const maxid = 4000
fr = FreeFile
Open "d:\temp\ids.txt" For Output As #fr
' Create temporary toolbar
Set cbar = oVBE.CommandBars.Add("temporary", msoBarTop, _
   False, True)
For i = 1 To maxid
   On Error Resume Next ' skip if cannot add
   cbar.Controls.Add Id:=i
Next i
On Error GoTo 0
For Each ctl In cbar.Controls
   Print #fr, ctl.Caption & " (" & ctl.Id & ")"
Next
cbar.Delete
Close #fr
```

Example 4-2 shows a small portion of the resulting file when the code is run on my system. Appendix A, *Built-in Command Bar Controls*, contains a complete list of control IDs.

Example 4-2. Outputting the IDs of Command Bar Controls

```
&Run (4)
&Outdent (14)
&Indent (15)
&Copy (19)
&Help (21)
&Paste (22)
&File (23)
Toggle Folders (32)
```

Example 4-2. Outputting the IDs of Command Bar Controls (continued)

```
He&lp (49)
&Toggle Breakpoint (51)
&Add-Ins (128)
&Window (129)
&Find... (141)
Add ActiveX Desi&gner (166)
&Toolbars (167)
&Start (186)
Step &Into (188)
Brea&k (189)
Comment Block (192)
```

We will consider an example that uses built-in controls in the later section "Example: Creating a Toolbar" (at which time it should become clearer just what a built-in control is.)

Example: Creating a Menu

Adding menu items (control buttons) to an existing VB menu is one way to give the user access to the features of the add-in. Personally, I prefer not to clutter up VB's menus, so instead I add a new popup menu to the main menu bar. Then I can add as many features as I like, placing all menu items under my custom menu.

Let's give this a try. You should key this code into your add-in shell project, because we will consider it to be part of the project from now on. The code simply creates the menu system shown in Figure 4-4 with a single menu item.

Figure 4-4. A simple menu system

The first step is to add some declarations to the Declarations section of the Connect class:

```
' For menu items
Private cbcCustom As Office.CommandBarControl
Private cbcFeature1 As Office.CommandBarControl
```

These variables are of type CommandBarControl, because that is what we are adding to the VB menu—one popup control and one button control. (Adding the popup control adds the menu.) Note also that these are private variables, since we will need them only in this class module, and we don't want them to be accessible to the rest of the world.

Next we add the private procedure in Example 4-3, which creates the two controls, to the Connect class module.

Example 4-3. The CreateCustomMenu Procedure

```
Private Sub CreateCustomMenu()

' Create popup control on the main menu bar
Set cbcCustom = oVBE.CommandBars("Menu bar"). _
   Controls.Add(Type:=msoControlPopup)

cbcCustom.Caption = "&Custom"

' Add a menu item (i.e. button control)
Set cbcFeature1 = cbcCustom.Controls.Add( _
   Type:=msoControlButton)

cbcFeature1.Caption = "Feature&1"

End Sub
```

There are a couple of things to notice about the code in Example 4-3. First, you will recall our earlier discussion of the Controls property of the CommandBar object and the Controls property of the CommandBarControl object of type CommandBarPopup. The code in Example 4-3 uses both properties to add new controls. Second, note the use of the ampersand character (&) in the Caption properties; it signals a hot key (or accelerator key). Thus, "&Custom" appears as Custom in the menu bar and can be invoked using the keystroke combination Alt-C.

To call this procedure from the OnConnection method, place the line:

```
    CreateCustomMenu
```

in this method.

Finally, to remove the menus when the add-in is deactivated, place the line:

```
    cbcCustom.Delete
```

in the OnDisconnection method.

Now you can try out the menus by starting the add-in project and activating the add-in from the client project.

Hooking the Menu's Click Event

This menu system is very nice, but it doesn't do anything. We need to provide a way for VB to tell us that the user has chosen the Feature1 menu item.

If we were adding this menu system to an Office application such as Microsoft Word, we could simply set the OnAction property of the cbcFeature1 control to the name of a Word macro.

However, here we need to go to a little bit more work, and this is where VBIDE objects come into play. In particular, the VB IDE object model provides a special CommandBarEvents object. There is a CommandBarEvents object for each command bar control. The CommandBarEvents object for the cbcFeature1 control is:

```
oVBE.Events.CommandBarEvents(cbcFeature1)
```

The CommandBarEvents object has a single method in its interface: the Click method. By declaring a variable of type CommandBarEvents using the **WithEvents** keyword, Visual Basic both fires the Click method when the menu item is clicked and provides us with an event code shell for this method. In other words, VB turns the Click method into a Click event into which we can place our code.

Thus, you should place the following declaration in the Declarations section of the Connect class:

```
Private WithEvents cbeFeature1 As CommandBarEvents
```

In the OnConnection method, after the call to *CreateCustomMenu*, we can set this variable equal to the CommandBarEvents object for the command bar control in question. This is sometimes called *hooking* the event.

```
Set cbeFeature1 = _
    oVBE.Events.CommandBarEvents(cbcFeature1)
```

The **WithEvents** statement causes VB to supply us with a Click event code shell, which we fill with a message box for now, as Example 4-4 shows.

Example 4-4. The Feature1 Button's Click Event

```
Private Sub cbeFeature1_Click( _
    ByVal CommandBarControl As Object, _
    handled As Boolean, _
    CancelDefault As Boolean)

MsgBox "Add-in Feature 1"

End Sub
```

The CommandBarControl parameter is filled with a reference to the control that caused the event, in this case the cbcFeature1 control. The other parameters can safely be ignored.

The Add-in Code Shell

After making these additions, the entire Connect class for our add-in code shell for VB5 appears as shown in Example 4-5. This constitutes the entire add-in code shell with the exception of the *AddToINI* subroutine in the **basMain** standard module. Similarly, the source code for the add-in shell's Connect class for VB6 appears in Example 4-6. (The add-in shell for VB6, of course, doesn't require that *AddToIni* be present in the code module, since the add-in relies on the registry rather than an initialization file.) Note that we have added a second menu item to the Custom menu. You will probably find as you experiment with various code that it's useful to have two menu items with which to play. (In fact, we will add two more menu items later.)

Example 4-5. The Connect Class for VB5

```
Option Explicit

Implements IDTExtensibility

' Menu items
Private cbcCustom As Office.CommandBarControl
Private cbcFeature1 As Office.CommandBarControl
Private cbcFeature2 As Office.CommandBarControl

' To hook menu events
Private WithEvents cbeFeature1 As CommandBarEvents
Private WithEvents cbeFeature2 As CommandBarEvents

'-----
Private Sub cbeFeature1_Click( _
   ByVal CommandBarControl As Object, _
   handled As Boolean, _
   CancelDefault As Boolean)

   MsgBox "Add-in Feature 1"

End Sub

'-----
Private Sub cbeFeature2_Click( _
   ByVal CommandBarControl As Object, _
   handled As Boolean, _
   CancelDefault As Boolean)

   MsgBox "Add-in Feature 2"

End Sub

'-----
Private Sub IDTExtensibility_OnConnection( _
   ByVal VBInst As Object, _
   ByVal ConnectMode As VBIDE.vbext_ConnectMode, _
   ByVal AddInInst As VBIDE.AddIn, _
   custom() As Variant)

   On Error GoTo ERROR_CONNECT

   ' Save the instance of VB
   Set oVBE = VBInst
```

Example 4-5. The Connect Class for VB5 (continued)

```
    ' Place code in following TEST AREA for testing
    ' objects of the VBIDE object model.
    '-----------------------------------------

    '-----------------------------------------

    ' Set breakpoint for testing.
    Debug.Print "*** Started " & Now & " ***"

    ' Make menu
    CreateCustomMenu
    ' Hook menu events
    Set cbeFeature1 = _
        oVBE.Events.CommandBarEvents(cbcFeature1)
    Set cbeFeature2 = _
        oVBE.Events.CommandBarEvents(cbcFeature2)

    Exit Sub

ERROR_CONNECT:

    MsgBox Err.Description

End Sub

'-----
Private Sub IDTExtensibility_OnDisconnection( _
  ByVal RemoveMode As VBIDE.vbext_DisconnectMode, _
  custom() As Variant)

cbcCustom.Delete
Debug.Print "*** Ended " & Now & " ***"

End Sub

'-----
Private Sub IDTExtensibility_OnStartupComplete( _
  custom() As Variant)
'
End Sub

'-----
Private Sub IDTExtensibility_OnAddInsUpdate( _
    custom() As Variant)
'
End Sub

'-----
Public Sub CreateCustomMenu()

' Create popup control on main menu bar
Set cbcCustom = oVBE.CommandBars("Menu bar"). _
```

Example 4-5. The Connect Class for VB5 (continued)

```
    Controls.Add(Type:=msoControlPopup)
cbcCustom.Caption = "&Custom"

' Add menu item
Set cbcFeature1 = cbcCustom.Controls.Add( _
    Type:=msoControlButton)
cbcFeature1.Caption = "Feature&1"

' Add menu item
Set cbcFeature2 = cbcCustom.Controls.Add( _
    Type:=msoControlButton)
cbcFeature2.Caption = "Feature&2"

End Sub
```

Example 4-6. The Connect Class for VB6

```
Option Explicit

' Menu items
Private cbcCustom As Office.CommandBarControl
Private cbcFeature1 As Office.CommandBarControl
Private cbcFeature2 As Office.CommandBarControl

' To hook menu events
Private WithEvents cbeFeature1 As CommandBarEvents
Private WithEvents cbeFeature2 As CommandBarEvents

'-----
Private Sub AddinInstance_OnAddInsUpdate(custom() _
                                        As Variant)

End Sub

'-----
Private Sub AddinInstance_OnBeginShutdown(custom() _
                                         As Variant)

End Sub

'-----
Private Sub AddinInstance_OnConnection(_
    ByVal Application As Object, _
    ByVal ConnectMode As AddInDesignerObjects.ext_ConnectMode, _
    ByVal AddInInst As Object, custom() As Variant)


    On Error GoTo ERROR_CONNECT

    ' Save the instance of VB
    Set oVBE = Application

    ' Place code in following TEST AREA for testing
```

Example 4-6. The Connect Class for VB6 (continued)

```
    ' objects of the VBIDE object model.
    '----------------------------------------


    '----------------------------------------


    ' Set breakpoint for testing.
    Debug.Print "*** Started " & Now & " ***"

    ' Make menu
    CreateCustomMenu
    ' Hook menu events
    Set cbeFeature1 = _
        oVBE.Events.CommandBarEvents(cbcFeature1)
    Set cbeFeature2 = _
        oVBE.Events.CommandBarEvents(cbcFeature2)

    Exit Sub

ERROR_CONNECT:

    MsgBox Err.Description

End Sub

'-----
Private Sub AddinInstance_OnDisconnection( _
 ByVal RemoveMode As AddInDesignerObjects.ext_DisconnectMode, _
    custom() As Variant)

cbcCustom.Delete
Debug.Print "*** Ended " & Now & " ***"

End Sub

'-----
Private Sub cbeFeature1_Click( _
    ByVal CommandBarControl As Object, _
    handled As Boolean, _
    CancelDefault As Boolean)

    MsgBox "Add-in Feature 1"

End Sub

'-----
Private Sub cbeFeature2_Click( _
    ByVal CommandBarControl As Object, _
    handled As Boolean, _
    CancelDefault As Boolean)

    MsgBox "Add-in Feature 2"
```

Example 4-6. The Connect Class for VB6 (continued)

```
End Sub

'-----
Public Sub CreateCustomMenu()

' Create popup control on main menu bar
Set cbcCustom = oVBE.CommandBars("Menu bar"). _
   Controls.Add(Type:=msoControlPopup)
cbcCustom.Caption = "&Custom"

' Add menu item
Set cbcFeature1 = cbcCustom.Controls.Add( _
   Type:=msoControlButton)
cbcFeature1.Caption = "Feature&1"

' Add menu item
Set cbcFeature2 = cbcCustom.Controls.Add( _
   Type:=msoControlButton)
cbcFeature2.Caption = "Feature&2"

End Sub
```

Example: A More Elaborate Menu

The following example shows how to add a submenu to our custom menuing system. The results are shown in Figure 4-5. We indicate only the changes required in the add-in code shell described above, and won't consider this as part of the basic add-in code shell.

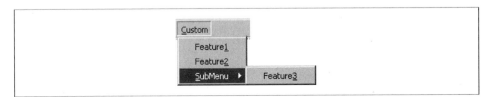

Figure 4-5. An example with a submenu

First, we need to add two more declarations to cover the Feature3 button control:

```
Private cbcFeature3 As Office.CommandBarControl
Private WithEvents cbeFeature3 As CommandBarEvents
```

We also need a new Click event for the second feature; its source code is shown in Example 4-7.

Example 4-7. The Feature3 Button's Click Event

```
Private Sub cbeFeature3_Click( _
  ByVal CommandBarControl As Object, _
```

Example 4-7. The Feature3 Button's Click Event (continued)

```
  handled As Boolean, _
  CancelDefault As Boolean)

MsgBox "Add-in Feature 3"

End Sub
```

The OnConnection method needs updating to hook the new menu item. Just add the line:

```
  Set cbeFeature3 = _
    oVBE.Events.CommandBarEvents(cbcFeature3)
```

Of course, there is a new *CreateCustomMenu* procedure; its source code listing appears in Example 4-8.

Example 4-8. The CreateCustomMenu Procedure

```
Public Sub CreateCustomMenu()

Dim cbsub As Office.CommandBarControl

' Create popup control on main menu bar
Set cbcCustom = oVBE.CommandBars("Menu bar"). _
  Controls.Add(Type:=msoControlPopup)
cbcCustom.Caption = "&Custom"

' Add menu item
Set cbcFeature1 = cbcCustom.Controls.Add( _
  Type:=msoControlButton)
cbcFeature1.Caption = "Feature&1"

' Add menu item
Set cbcFeature2 = cbcCustom.Controls.Add( _
  Type:=msoControlButton)
cbcFeature2.Caption = "Feature&2"

' Add popup for a submenu
Set cbsub = _
  cbcCustom.Controls.Add(Type:=msoControlPopup)
cbsub.Caption = "&SubMenu"

' Add menu item to submenu
Set cbcFeature3 = _
  cbsub.Controls.Add(Type:=msoControlButton)
cbcFeature3.Caption = "Feature&3"

End Sub
```

Example: Creating a Toolbar

Let's construct a custom toolbar for our add-in with three different types of controls, as shown in Figure 4-6. This illustrates the use of VB's built-in command controls as well. We will *not* consider this as part of the basic add-in code shell.

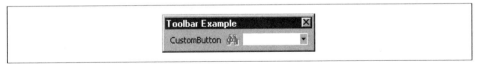

Figure 4-6. A custom toolbar

The first step is to place some additional declarations in the Declarations section of the Connect class module:

```
' Toolbar items
Private cbCustom As Office.CommandBar
Private cbcFeature3 As Office.CommandBarControl
Private cbcListBox As Office.CommandBarControl

' To hook toolbar events
Private WithEvents cbeFeature3 As CommandBarEvents
Private WithEvents cbeListBox As CommandBarEvents
```

We also need new Click events for the custom button (on the left) and the list box, but not for the built-in button control. Example 4-9 shows the source code for the two Click events.

Example 4-9. The cbeFeature3 and cbeListBox Buttons' Click Events

```
Private Sub cbeFeature3_Click( _
  ByVal CommandBarControl As Object, _
  handled As Boolean, _
  CancelDefault As Boolean)

MsgBox "Add-in Feature 3 - Custom Toolbar Button"

End Sub

Private Sub cbeListBox_Click( _
  ByVal CommandBarControl As Object, _
  handled As Boolean, _
  CancelDefault As Boolean)

MsgBox "You chose " & _
  cbcListBox.List(cbcListBox.ListIndex)

End Sub
```

Next, we add a call to the *CreateCustomToolbar* procedure and hooks to the custom button and list box to the OnConnection method:

```
CreateCustomToolbar
Set cbeFeature3 = _
  oVBE.Events.CommandBarEvents(cbcFeature3)
Set cbeListBox = _
  oVBE.Events.CommandBarEvents(cbcListBox)
```

The add-in will need to call the Delete method of the *cbCustom* toolbar in the OnDisconnection method:

```
cbCustom.Delete
```

Now we are ready for the *CreateCustomToolbar* procedure, which is shown in Example 4-10.

Example 4-10. The CreateCustomToolbar Procedure

```
Sub CreateCustomToolbar()

Dim cbctl As Office.CommandBarControl

' Create a floating toolbar
Set cbCustom = oVBE.CommandBars.Add( _
  Name:="Toolbar Example", _
  Position:=msoBarFloating)
cbCustom.Visible = True

' Add a custom button control
Set cbcFeature3 = cbCustom.Controls.Add( _
  Type:=msoControlButton)

' The following is needed for caption
cbcFeature3.Style = msoButtonCaption
cbcFeature3.Caption = "CustomButton"

' Add built-in Find... control
Set cbctl = cbCustom.Controls.Add(Id:=141)
' Icon for button
cbctl.FaceId = 141

' Add a list box
Set cbcListBox = cbCustom.Controls.Add( _
  Type:=msoControlDropdown)

' Set list properties of the list box
With cbcListBox
    .Caption = "Composers"
    .AddItem "Chopin", 1
    .AddItem "Mozart", 2
    .AddItem "Bach", 3
    .DropDownLines = 0
    .DropDownWidth = 75
    ' select nothing to start
    .ListIndex = 0
End With

End Sub
```

The first line of the procedure creates a floating toolbar whose name is "Toolbar Example." Next, we add a custom button control (its *Id* argument is missing) and a built-in Find... custom control, whose *Id* happens to be 141. (We have already discussed how to get built-in control IDs.) This custom control automatically displays the Find dialog box, so we don't need to hook its Click event. Note that the *FaceId* is also set to 141. This displays the default icon (binoculars), but we could have chosen another built-in control icon if desired, by selecting a different face ID number.

Finally, we add a custom list box and populate it with the names of three composers. The Click event for this control simply displays the user's choice.

Example: Adding an Item to an Existing Menu

Of course, rather than creating a custom toolbar or adding a custom menu to the Visual Basic idea, you may prefer to add a button to an existing toolbar or a menu item to an existing menu. In that case, you simply need to retrieve a reference to the CommandBarControl object to which you wish to add the item and call the Controls collection's Add method. Example 4-11, which contains the complete source code for a very simple add-in that displays the VBA version number, shows how this can be done. It installs a VBA Version menu item immediately before the About Microsoft Visual Basic option on the Help menu. Note that the add-in is able to determine the precise location of the About menu option by retrieving a reference to its CommandBarControl object.

Example 4-11. Adding an Item to an Existing Menu

```
Option Explicit

Private objMenuItem As Office.CommandBarControl
Private WithEvents objeMenuItem As CommandBarEvents

Private Sub AddinInstance_OnConnection(_
    ByVal Application As Object, _
    ByVal ConnectMode As AddInDesignerObjects.ext_ConnectMode, _
    ByVal AddInInst As Object, custom() As Variant)

Dim objHelpMenu As Office.CommandBarControl
Dim objPrevItem As Office.CommandBarControl

Set oVBE = Application
Set objHelpMenu = oVBE.CommandBars("Menu Bar").Controls("&Help")
Set objPrevItem = objHelpMenu.Controls(_
                "&About Microsoft Visual Basic...")
Set objMenuItem = objHelpMenu.Controls.Add( _
                Type:=msoControlButton, _
```

Example 4-11. Adding an Item to an Existing Menu (continued)

```
                    Temporary:=True, _
                    Before:=objPrevItem.Index)

objMenuItem.Caption = "VBA Version"
objMenuItem.BeginGroup = True

Set objeMenuItem = _
    oVBE.Events.CommandBarEvents(objMenuItem)

End Sub

Private Sub AddinInstance_OnDisconnection(_
            ByVal RemoveMode As AddInDesignerObjects.ext_DisconnectMode, _
            custom() As Variant)

Set objeMenuItem = Nothing
objMenuItem.Delete

End Sub

Private Sub objeMenuItem_Click( _
            ByVal CommandBarControl As Object, _
            handled As Boolean, _
            CancelDefault As Boolean)

MsgBox "VBA Version " & oVBE.Version, _
        vbInformation Or vbOKOnly, _
        "Version Information"

End Sub
```

Built-in Face IDs

If you would like to see the various icons used in the built-in button controls and get their face IDs, just place the code shown in Example 4-12 in your add-in and add a call to it to the test area. Note that this code creates 13 custom toolbars and fills them with all the built-in button controls. Since the toolbars are temporary, they will go away when you shut down the client project. (If for some reason they don't, just right-click the VB menu bar and choose Customize. Then you can delete the toolbars from the Toolbars tab.) Note also that this program may take some time to run. You may prefer to test it first by reducing the upper limit of the For bars = loop to 2.

Example 4-12. Showing the Icons Used in the Built-in Button Controls

```
Sub ShowFaceIDs()

Const max = 4000
Dim bars As Integer, i As Integer
Dim firstID As Integer, lastId As Integer
Dim tb As Office.CommandBar
```

Example 4-12. Showing the Icons Used in the Built-in Button Controls (continued)

```
Dim btn As Office.CommandBarControl
On Error GoTo PastLastButton

For bars = 0 To 13
    firstID = bars * 300
    lastId = firstID + 299
    Set tb = oVBE.CommandBars.Add( _
      Name:=CStr(firstID) & "-" & CStr(lastId), _
      Temporary:=True)

    For i = firstID To lastId
      If i >= 3519 Then GoTo PastLastButton
      Set btn = tb.Controls.Add
      btn.FaceId = i
      btn.ToolTipText = "FaceID " & i
    Next

    tb.Visible = True
    tb.Width = 591
Next
PastLastButton:
End Sub
```

The output is shown in Figure 4-7. All icons are shown in Appendix B, *Face IDs*.

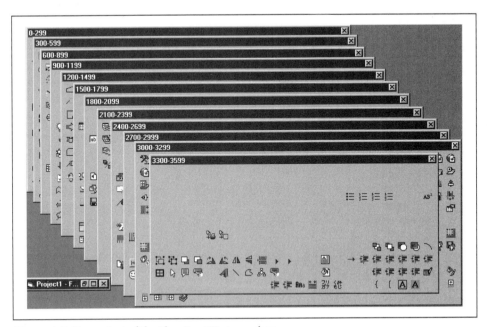

Figure 4-7. The output of the ShowFaceIDs procedure

In this chapter:
- *Setting Break Points in an Add-in*
- *Getting Information from a Running Add-in*

5

Debugging Add-ins

Unfortunately, VB doesn't allow us to debug an add-in by placing it in the client project (as can be done with ordinary ActiveX DLLs). This creates certain problems, chief among which are:

- Message boxes that are displayed from the add-in may not be visible from the client

- Certain statements, such as *SendKeys*, won't work out-of-process

In fact, when something isn't working and you suspect the problem might be the process boundary, it's worth testing the code from a compiled DLL.

Setting Break Points in an Add-in

VB does allow break points to be set in add-in code. Let's try an example, so you can see what to expect.

First, set a breakpoint in the add-in shell project at the `Debug.Print` line in the OnConnection method. Then run the project. Switch to the client project and activate the add-in from the Add-In Manager. You should be taken to the add-in project and placed in break mode at the `Debug.Print` line.

Go to the add-in project's Immediate window and enter the line

```
? oVBE.VBProjects(1).Name
```

The response should be:

```
Project1
```

What to Do from Break Mode

Let's assume that an add-in is in break mode, either because we set a breakpoint or because VB has stopped execution at a runtime error. When we are done fiddling, how do we proceed?

If there are no errors, we can simply continue running the add-in (hit F5). However, if there is an error, execution can't continue. To fix it, there are two choices:

- A first thought would probably be to return to the client project and deactivate the add-in. However, VB won't let us do that, because the add-in is in break mode and is therefore not responding to the client. In fact, anything we do in the client project generates the message box shown in Figure 5-1. Thus, the client can be of no help when the add-in is in break mode.

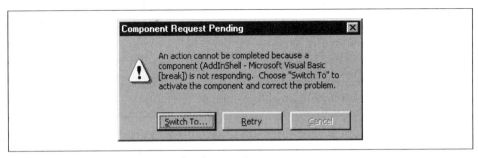

Figure 5-1. Attempting to activate the client project

However, attempting to terminate an add-in that is in break mode before deactivating that add-in from the client project produces the dialog box shown in Figure 5-2. Thus, to terminate the add-in, we risk causing some problems to the client. The most common problem occurs when the add-in creates menu items in the client IDE. These items should normally be removed by code that we place in the OnDisconnection method of the add-in. However, if the add-in is summarily deactivated, the OnDisconnection method isn't fired and the menu items will remain.

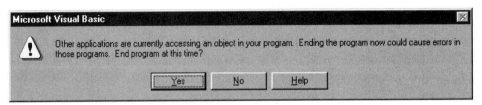

Figure 5-2. Attempting to terminate an add-in in break mode

Fortunately, VB makes it easy to clean up orphaned menu and toolbar items. We just right click on VB's top menu bar and select Customize. As long as the

Customize dialog box is open, we can use the mouse to drag unwanted menu and toolbar items off of their containers and into oblivion.

- A better alternative to terminating an active add-in is to alter the program flow so the add-in can be allowed to finish execution. This can be done by simply using the Set Next Statement feature (which is available as an option on the Debug menu, or simply by dragging the execution arrow to the next statement to be executed) to move execution past the offending problem (perhaps to an **Exit Sub** statement).

From time to time, you may also run into the dialog box shown in Figure 5-3. This can be caused by an error in the OnConnection method that causes termination of the add-in. The client's Add-In Manager is trying to activate the add-in, but not having any luck. Therefore, it offers the choice of removing the reference to the add-in within the *vbaddin.ini* file or the registry (in VB6). Unless we intend to abandon the add-in completely, the proper response to this dialog box is No.

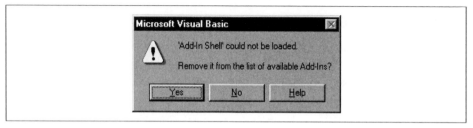

Figure 5-3. An add-in can't be loaded

Getting Information from a Running Add-in

There are many situations in which we need to get messages from a running add-in. This can be done in a variety of ways:

- Displaying a message box
- Using **Debug.Print**
- Using audio signals (beep codes)
- Displaying information in the client's VB IDE

As we have seen, message boxes can be annoying and can't be relied upon to provide asynchronous error information. In other words, we can't rely on a message box to interrupt us at the right time if it's hidden behind other windows.

Similarly, the use of the **Debug.Print** statement is hampered considerably by the fact that the message appears in the add-in's Immediate window, which, of course, is only available in the design-time environment.

Beep Codes

One very simple way to get feedback from an add-in is to insert code that causes the PC's speaker to beep. In fact, I often use the `Beep` statement to return *beep codes* (one or more beeps in quick succession) that give me information without having to display message boxes or switch applications.

You might want to add the *Beeps* procedure shown in Example 5-1 to the *basMain* module in your add-in code shell.

Example 5-1. The Beeps Procedure

```
Public Sub Beeps(iTimes As Integer)
Dim i As Integer
For i = 1 To iTimes: Beep: Next
End Sub
```

You can then insert beep codes in your add-ins (or in other programs as well).

Printing to the Client's Immediate Window

The `Debug.Print` statement prints information to the Immediate window of the add-in. However, the PrintToDebug procedure shown in Example 5-2 prints text messages to the Immediate window of the client, assuming that this window is visible. You can also add it to the *basMain* module. (It only works from within an add-in, since it requires access to the VB IDE object model.)

Example 5-2. The PrintToDebug Procedure

```
Sub PrintToDebug(sText As String)

' Print sText to Immediate window of client

Dim wActive As Window
Dim wImm As Window

' Save active window
Set wActive = oVBE.ActiveWindow

' Reference to Immediate window
Set wImm = oVBE.Windows("Immediate")

' If none, then exit
If wImm Is Nothing Then Exit Sub

' Proceed only if visible
If wImm.Visible = True Then
  wImm.SetFocus
  SendKeys "^({End})", True
  SendKeys sText, True
End If
```

Example 5-2. The PrintToDebug Procedure (continued)

```
' Restore original focus
wActive.SetFocus

End Sub
```

To print an item to the Immediate window of the client, place this line in the add-in:

```
PrintToDebug "message goes here"
```

This approach still has one drawback. Since it uses the **SendKeys** statement, it works only when the add-in is being run as an in-process DLL (not when tested out of process). To use it during testing, we need to compile and test the actual DLL.

ToolWindows

There is another solution to getting information from a running add-in that involves an add-in feature called a *ToolWindow*. ToolWindow objects are special IDE windows that can be created by add-ins and appear in the IDE. Moreover, a ToolWindow acts like a built-in VB IDE window, such as the Properties window, in the sense that it's nonmodal, stays on top of other windows, and can even be docked!

I'd normally not bring up ToolWindows until later (if at all), but since it will prove useful for testing other add-in code, we will discuss the steps required to create a ToolWindow now.

This ToolWindow is handy, and I'd suggest creating it. However, if for some reason you prefer not to create this ToolWindow, you can substitute a *MsgBox* function, a call to the **Debug.Print** statement, or the use of the *PrintToDebug* procedure discussed earlier. In any case, the steps required to create the ToolWindow are as follows:

1. *Creating the ToolWindow object*

   A ToolWindow is a window that contains an ActiveX document; that is, a User Document. So the first step is to create this object.

   Add a User Document module to the add-in shell project and name it *docMessages*. Place a list box on the user document and name it *lstMessages*. The code for the user document is shown in the code below. There is some resizing code, along with three public methods—one to add an item to the list box, one to clear the list box, and one to do both.

   ```
   Option Explicit

   Private Sub UserDocument_Resize()
   lstMessages.Width = ScaleWidth - (lstMessages.Left * 2)
   lstMessages.Height = ScaleHeight - 100
   ```

```
End Sub

Public Sub AddItem(sText As String)
lstMessages.AddItem sText
End Sub

Public Sub Clear(sText As String)
lstMessages.Clear
End Sub

Public Sub FirstItem(sText As String)
lstMessages.Clear
lstMessages.AddItem sText
End Sub
```

2. *Declaring the ToolWindow in the add-in*

   In the Declarations section of *basMain*, place the declarations shown below:

```
' The ToolWindow
Public gwinWindow As VBIDE.Window
' The UserDocument returned to us
Public aiMsg As Object
```

3. *Generating a GUID*

   We need a globally unique identifier (GUID) to identify the ToolWindow. Microsoft provides a utility called *GUIDGEN.EXE* (which should be on your VB5 CD-ROM) to generate this number. (If necessary, you can use the GUID in this example, but it's better to generate your own.)

   After starting *GUIDGEN.EXE*, the dialog box shown in Figure 5-4 should appear. Make sure choice 4 is selected and hit the Copy button.

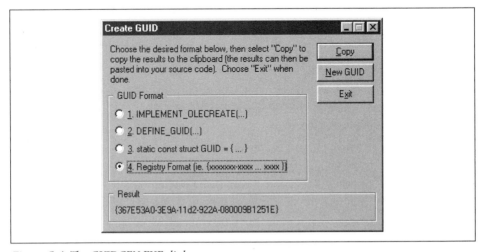

Figure 5-4. The GUIDGEN.EXE dialog

In the Connect class, add the following declaration:

```
Const sGUID = "{3265F830-FD84-11d1-8B8B-000000000000}"
```

substituting your GUID, which is now on the Clipboard.

4. *Create the ToolWindow*

In the OnConnection method, place the code shown below, which creates the ToolWindow using the CreateToolWindow method of the Windows collection:

```
' Save active window
Dim winActive As Window
Set winActive = oVBE.ActiveWindow

' Create ToolWindow
Set gwinWindow = oVBE.Windows.CreateToolWindow( _
   AddInInst, "AddInShell.docMessages", _
   "Add-In Messages", sGUID, aiMsg)

' Make it visible
gwinWindow.Visible = True

' Return focus
If Not winActive Is Nothing Then winActive.SetFocus
```

Let's pause briefly to discuss the syntax of this method, which is:

```
WindowsObject.CreateToolWindow(AddInInst, ProgId, _
            Caption, GuidPosition, DocObj) As Window
```

The *AddInInst* parameter is the add-in in which to create the ToolWindow. Fortunately, this is passed to us by VB as one of the parameters of the OnConnection method. The *ProgID* parameter is set to the programmatic ID of the UserDocument object, which is:

```
AddInShell.docMessages
```

(Recall that the *ProgID* has the form *ProjectName.ClassName*.) The *Caption* parameter should be set to the caption for the UserDocument. The *GuidPosition* parameter is the GUID we prepared in the previous step for the ToolWindow. Finally, *DocObj* is an object variable that should be declared **As Object** and that will be filled by VB with a reference to the UserDocument (ActiveX document) created by this method. The method returns the Window object that is created.

5. *Destroying object references*

Finally, and very importantly, we must destroy all references to objects in the OnDisconnection method:

```
Set aiMsg = Nothing
Set gwinWindow = Nothing
```

If we fail to do this, part of the add-in will remain in memory after the add-in is disconnected. The only recourse at that point is to close all instances of VB.

6. *Testing the ToolWindow*

Let's give the ToolWindow a try. Place the following code in the Click event of cbeFeature1:

```
aiMsg.AddItem Now
```

Now run the add-in project. Switch to the client project and activate the add-in. You should see a new window, as in Figure 5-5. Moreover, each time the Feature1 menu item is selected, a new timestamp should appear in the window.

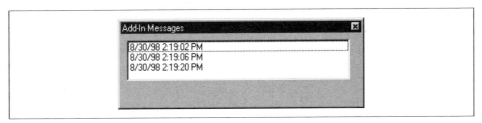

Figure 5-5. The ToolWindow

I have noticed a couple of potential problems with the ToolWindow. First, on some systems, if you deactivate the add-in, the focus may appear to get lost, and the VB menu seems not to respond to the keyboard. If this happens, use the mouse to activate the VB menu bar or set the focus on the Project window using Ctrl+R. You can also switch to and from another application (Alt+Tab).

Second, if the ToolWindow has the focus, the VB IDE doesn't seem to respond very well (if at all). For our purposes (displaying messages), this window need never have the focus. If you should click on that window, just click on a different window to regain control over VB.

Incidentally, when you no longer want the ToolWindow, comment out the code in the OnConnection method that creates the window. Then if, at a later date, you need to use the ToolWindow, you can just uncomment the code.

II

The Extensibility Model

In this chapter:
* *The VBE and Parent Properties*
* *Properties and Methods of the VBE Object*
* *VB IDE Objects*

6

Overview of the Object Model

We now come to the heart of add-in programming—the Microsoft Visual Basic Extensibility Object Model, or VB IDE object model. The VB IDE object model is a relatively small model as far as Microsoft object models go, with about 50 objects, 250 properties, 150 methods, and 22 enums (with 179 constants).

Incidentally, the VB5 and VB6 object models (*vb5ext.olb* and *vb6ext.olb*) are essentially identical. The VB6 object model does have one additional object—VBBuildEvents. However, it is hidden, and there is no documentation for this event, so we can suppose that Microsoft doesn't want us to use this object anyway.

Figure 6-1 shows the top portion of the VB IDE object model. We have separated the IDTExtensibility object from the rest of the model because it's not accessible from the top-level VBE object.

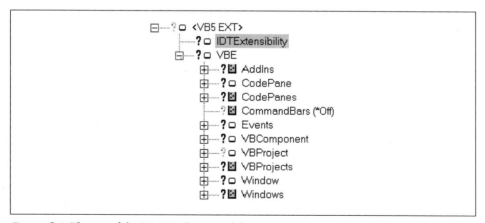

Figure 6-1. The top of the VB IDE object model

Figure 6-1 comes from an object browser, written by me, a coupon for which is included at the back of this book. The question marks in front of an object indicate that help is available from Microsoft's help files (usually). The small basket means that the object is a collection. Noncollection objects are indicate by small ovals. A plus sign following the object means that the object has children that aren't currently showing. The figure also shows that the VBE object has a total of 10 children, but the CommandBars child object belongs to the Microsoft Office object model.

The VBE and Parent Properties

You should note that virtually every object in the VB IDE object model has a VBE property that simply returns the top VBE object in the model. Thus, I'll say no more about this property. Similarly, about one-half of the objects in the VB IDE object model have a Parent property that returns the parent object. For instance, the parent of a VBForm object is the VB component that contains the VBForm object. We won't discuss the Parent property further.

Properties and Methods of the VBE Object

The list below shows the members (properties and methods) of the VBE object. (All the entries in this list are properties except Quit, which is a method.) We discuss the various members in the remaining chapters.

ActiveCodePane	Events	SelectedVBComponent
ActiveVBProject	FullName	TemplatePath
ActiveWindow	LastUsedPath	VBProjects
Addins	MainWindow	Version
CodePanes	Name	Windows
CommandBars	Quit	
DisplayModel	ReadOnlyMode	

VB IDE Objects

The objects in the VB IDE object model can be grouped into six categories:

- Objects that manipulate the VB IDE
- Objects that manipulate VB projects
- Objects that manipulate forms and controls
- Objects that provide access to events

- Objects that manipulate VB code

- Objects that manipulate add-ins

Figure 6-2 shows an expanded view of the VB IDE object model that captures much of its design. The plus signs in this figure indicate that the object has children that aren't shown in the diagram. The main portion of the object model that's missing from Figure 6-2 is its VBForms component, shown in Figure 6-3.

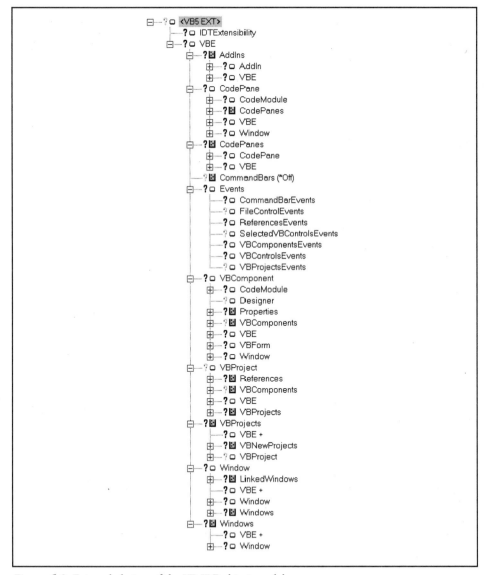

Figure 6-2. Expanded view of the VB IDE object model

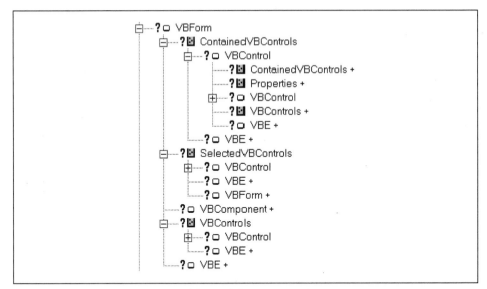

Figure 6-3. The VBForms portion of the model

7

User Interface Objects

In this chapter, we take a look at the objects that relate to the VB IDE's user interface. As shown in Figure 7-1, the principal objects are:

- CodePane and CodePanes

- CommandBar and CommandBars

- Window and Windows

We discussed CommandBars at length in an earlier chapter, so we will look at the other objects here.

The Window Object

Simply put, a Window object represents a window in the VB IDE. The VB IDE object model lets us do the following to a VB IDE window:

- Resize it

- Move it

- Make it visible or invisible

- Read (but not write) its caption

- Dock it to a linked window frame or link it to another window

The ActiveWindow property of the VBE object returns a reference to the currently active window (the window that has the focus when VB has the focus), as in:

```
Dim w as Window
Set w = oVBE.ActiveWindow
```

The MainWindow property returns a reference to the main VB IDE window:

```
Dim w as Window
Set w = oVBE.MainWindow
```

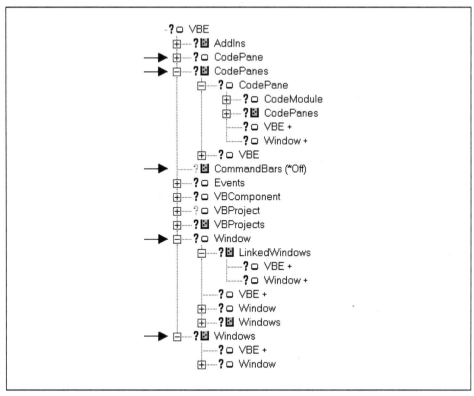

Figure 7-1. Objects related to the user interface

A Window object has twelve properties and two methods (*Close* and *SetFocus*), all of which are shown in the following list:

Caption	LinkedWindowFrame	VBE
Close	LinkedWindows	Visible
Collection	SetFocus	Width
Height	Top	WindowState
Left	Type	

Let's take a look at some of these members.

The Type Property

The read-only Type property of a Window object describes the type of the window. Its value can be any one of the constants in the following **vbext_WindowType** enum:

```
Enum vbext_WindowType
    vbext_wt_CodeWindow = 0
```

```
            vbext_wt_Designer = 1
            vbext_wt_Browser = 2
            vbext_wt_Watch = 3
            vbext_wt_Locals = 4
            vbext_wt_Immediate = 5
            vbext_wt_ProjectWindow = 6
            vbext_wt_PropertyWindow = 7
            vbext_wt_Find = 8
            vbext_wt_FindReplace = 9
            vbext_wt_Toolbox = 10
            vbext_wt_LinkedWindowFrame = 11
            vbext_wt_MainWindow = 12
            vbext_wt_Preview = 13
            vbext_wt_ColorPalette = 14
            vbext_wt_ToolWindow = 15
        End Enum
```

In a more general sense, Window objects fall into two categories, which Microsoft refers to as:

- Code windows and designers (windows of type 0 or 1)
- Development environment windows (the rest)

We will refer to code windows and designers as temporary windows (for reasons that will become clear in a moment) and the other types of windows as permanent windows.

The Windows Collection

The Windows collection contains all the IDE's Window objects, both permanent and temporary. *Permanent windows* can't be removed from the Windows collection. Applying the Close method just makes the window invisible; that is, it has the same effect as setting the Visible property to **True**.

On the other hand, *temporary windows* come and go from the Windows collection. The Close method can remove a temporary window from the Windows collection. (Setting the Visible property of a temporary window to **False** simply makes the window invisible.)

Note that we don't create new windows directly; the Windows collection has no Add method. Instead, we activate a particular VB component (form or module), which causes VB to create a Window object for that component. We discuss the Activate method of the VBComponent object in Chapter 8, *Project-Related Objects*.

Nonetheless, if a window is in the Windows collection, we refer to it as an *open window*. This has significance only for temporary windows, since permanent windows are always open.

Access to the Windows collection is available through the Windows property of
the VBE object, as in:

```
Dim ws as Windows
Set ws = oVBE.Windows
MsgBox ws.Count
```

For example, to display a list of the currently open windows, that is, the windows
in the Windows collection, along with their types, just place the code in
Example 7-1 in the Click event of the Feature1 control in your add-in code shell.

Example 7-1. Listing Currently Open Windows

```
Private Sub cbeFeature1_Click( _
   ByVal CommandBarControl As Object, _
   handled As Boolean, _
   CancelDefault As Boolean)

' Display window captions and types
aiMsg.FirstItem "CAPTION -- TYPE"
For Each w In oVBE.Windows
   s = IIf(w.Caption <> "", w.Caption, _
     "(none)") & " // " & WindowTypeName(w.Type)
   aiMsg.AddItem s
Next

End Sub
```

The *WindowTypeName* procedure used above simply converts a number (the
value of a Window object's Type property) into a symbolic constant. Its source
code is shown in Example 7-2. You can place this procedure in the standard
basMain module.

Example 7-2. The WindowTypeName Procedure

```
Function WindowTypeName(iValue As Integer) _
  As String

Dim sName As String
Select Case iValue
    Case 0: sName = "vbext_wt_CodeWindow"
    Case 1: sName = "vbext_wt_Designer"
    Case 2: sName = "vbext_wt_Browser"
    Case 3: sName = "vbext_wt_Watch"
    Case 4: sName = "vbext_wt_Locals"
    Case 5: sName = "vbext_wt_Immediate"
    Case 6: sName = "vbext_wt_ProjectWindow"
    Case 7: sName = "vbext_wt_PropertyWindow"
    Case 8: sName = "vbext_wt_Find"
    Case 9: sName = "vbext_wt_FindReplace"
    Case 10: sName = "vbext_wt_Toolbox"
    Case 11: sName = "vbext_wt_LinkedWindowFrame"
    Case 12: sName = "vbext_wt_MainWindow"
    Case 13: sName = "vbext_wt_Preview"
```

Example 7-2. The WindowTypeName Procedure (continued)

```
   Case 14: sName = "vbext_wt_ColorPalette"
   Case 15: sName = "vbext_wt_ToolWindow"
   Case Else: sName = "<invalid>"
End Select
WindowTypeName = sName
End Function
```

To refer to an existing window, we can use the window's caption as the index for the Item method. Thus, for instance, the window state for the Object Browser window is accessed as follows:

```
oVBE.Windows("Object Browser").WindowState
```

Window Size, Position, and State

The WindowState property can set or return the current state of the window. Its value comes from the following enum:

```
Enum vbext_WindowState
    vbext_ws_Normal = 0
    vbext_ws_Minimize = 1
    vbext_ws_Maximize = 2
End Enum
```

The Window object has the usual Left, Top, Height, and Width properties, which can be set in order to resize and reposition the window. Note that, contrary to what the help documentation states, these dimensions are measured in pixels, not twips.

The values of the Left, Top, Height, and Width properties of hidden windows are set to 0.

Linked and Docked Windows

As you know, some VB IDE windows can be *docked*; that is, attached to the edge of the main VB window. Some windows can also be *linked* to another window, which means attached to the side of another window.

All docked or linked windows lie inside a *linked window frame*, which is just a special type of window. To get the linked window frame of a window, we use the LinkedWindowFrame property. If a window isn't currently linked or docked, this property returns `Nothing`. To illustrate, consider the following modification of the code in Example 7-1:

```
aiMsg.FirstItem "CAPTION // TYPE // LINKED"

For Each w In oVBE.Windows

    s = IIf(w.Caption <> "", w.Caption, _
      "(none)")
```

```
s = s & " // " & WindowTypeName(w.Type) & " // "

If w.LinkedWindowFrame Is Nothing Then
    s = s & "(not linked)"
Else
    s = s & w.LinkedWindowFrame.Caption
End If

aiMsg.AddItem s

Next
```

Running this code when the window configuration is as shown in Figure 7-2 gives the output shown in Figure 7-3.

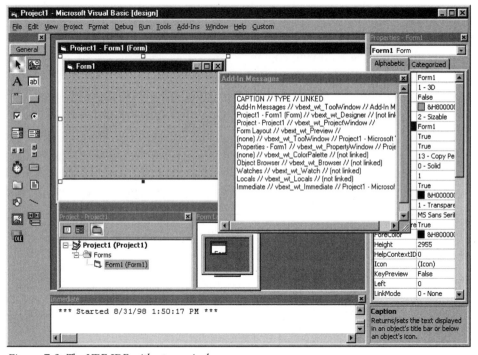

Figure 7-2. The VBE IDE with open windows

From these figures we can see, for instance, that the Properties window is docked to the main VB window, the form window isn't docked (or linked), and the Project and Form Layout windows are docked, but to a linked frame window that has no caption. (Nor can we set the caption, since it's read-only.)

A window can be docked to a linked window frame window by adding the window to the linked window frame window's LinkedWindows collection, using the Add method. For example, the following code (which could be placed in the usual Click event) causes the Form Layout window to be docked against the main VB IDE window:

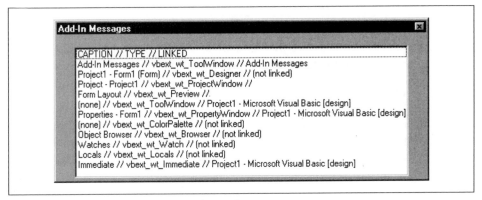

Figure 7-3. Linked windows in a WindowLinkFrame

```
For Each w In oVBE.Windows
    If w.Caption = "Form Layout" Then
        oVBE.MainWindow.LinkedWindows.Add w
    End If
Next
```

Similarly, the Remove method of the LinkedWindows collection undocks the window, but doesn't destroy it.

The problem with docking windows programmatically is that there does not seem to be any way to control the location of newly docked windows within the linked window frame. Thus, it may simply be better to let the user do her own docking with the mouse.

The CodePane Object

As you may know, a code window can be split into two separate *code panes*, using the split bar that lies above the vertical scroll bar in a code window. Thus, a code window may contain one or two code panes.

Exactly one of the code panes in a code window is *active*. It's the code pane that contains the cursor when the corresponding window has the input focus. The data in the Objects and Procedures list boxes located above the code window reflects the information in the active code pane.

The VBE object has a read-only ActiveCodePane property that returns the active CodePane object. Since the property is read-only, it can't set the active code pane.

Note that the F6 function key switches between code panes in a two-pane window; the active code pane can be changed this way using the SendKeys statement. As we will see, the Show method can cycle the active code pane through the entire CodePanes collection.

The CodePanes Collection

The VBE object also has a CodePanes property that returns a CodePanes collection. This collection contains all the *open* CodePane objects; that is, all the code panes that are associated with open code windows (whether visible or not). These are the code panes associated with the code windows that are currently in the Windows collection.

The CodePanes collection is rather boring, in the sense that we can't add or delete items from it. All we can do is access individual items by index number using the Item method and get a count of the total number of items in the collection (using the Count property).

Evidently, the CodePane objects that are associated with a code Window object aren't directly accessible from that Window object. (We might have expected a CodePanes collection for each Window object, containing one or two code panes.)

To find the CodePane object(s) that are associated with a given Window object, we must work backwards. That is, we can iterate through the CodePanes collection, checking the Window property (which returns the associated Window object) as we go.

CodePane Properties and Methods

The properties and methods of the CodePane object are given in the following list:

CodeModule	GetSelection	VBE
CodePaneView	SetSelection	Window
Collection	Show	
CountOfVisibleLines	TopLine	

The CodeModule property

We discuss CodeModule objects in Chapter 11, *Code-Related Objects*. Suffice it to say now that these important objects represent the actual code within a code pane.

The CodePaneView property

This property returns a value that indicates whether the code pane is in Procedure view or Full Module view. In particular, it takes on one of the values in the following enum:

```
Enum vbext_CodePaneview
    vbext_cv_ProcedureView = 0
    vbext_cv_FullModuleView = 1
End Enum
```

Unfortunately, this property is read-only, so we can't change the view state by setting this value. (Drat!)

The CountOfVisibleLines property

This read-only property returns a Long that gives the *maximum* number of visible lines possible in the code pane. This is the number of lines that would be visible if the code pane was completely full. (Thus, this property has nothing to do with the current code in the code pane.)

The TopLine property

This property returns or sets (as a Long) the line number of the line currently at the top of the code pane.

To experiment with this property, you can place the following line in the usual Click event of your AddInShell add-in:

```
oVBE.ActiveCodePane.TopLine = _
    InputBox("Enter top line number.")
```

There are a few points that should be made with respect to this property. First, the "lowest" view possible is when the last line in the code pane is at the *bottom* of the window, not the top (assuming there is enough code to fill the window). This view is obtained, for example, if we set the TopLine property to a number that is greater than the actual number of lines in the code pane. Because of this, the actual value of the TopLine property may be less than the value you assign to it. If it's important to know which line is at the top of a pane, you should retrieve the value of the TopLine property immediately after you assign a value to it.

Second, the TopLine setting is made relative to *all* of the code in the code pane, not just the visible code in the current procedure. Thus, line 1 is the first line in the Declarations section, even when the code pane is in Procedure view.

Finally, setting the TopLine property does not move the cursor. Thus, for instance, if the cursor is on line 100, we set the TopLine property to 1, and hit the down-arrow key, VB jumps to line 101! To avoid this, we must use the SetSelection method (discussed below) to move the cursor after setting the TopLine property.

The Show method

The Show method makes the code pane active; that is, it gives the code pane the focus. This makes it easy to cycle through all of the currently open code panes:

```
Static cCP As Integer

On Error Resume Next

' Validation
If cCP = 0 Then cCP = 1
If cCP > oVBE.CodePanes.Count Then cCP = 1

oVBE.CodePanes(cCP).Show
cCP = cCP + 1
```

The GetSelection and SetSelection methods

The GetSelection and SetSelection methods get and set the currently selected code within a code pane. The syntax for the SetSelection method is:

```
CodePaneObject.SetSelection(startline, startcol, endline, endcol)
```

where each of the parameters is a Long that specifies the starting or ending line or column of the selection.

Note that *startcol* pertains only to the first line of the selection, and *endcol* pertains only to the last line of the selection. Put another way, all lines in the selection except possibly the first and last are selected in their entirety.

Note also that the character at column *endcol* of line *endline* isn't included in the selection.

Thus, for instance, the code:

```
oVBE.ActiveCodePane.SetSelection 1, 4, 6, 3
```

selects line 1 starting in column 4, all of lines 2 through 5, and the first two character positions in line 6.

The GetSelection method is similar in syntax:

```
CodePaneObject.GetSelection(startline, startcol, endline, endcol)
```

The parameters have the same meaning as in the SetSelection method but are so-called *out parameters* (or arguments passed by reference to the method) because VB fills them with the correct values. However, we must declare the variables for VB, as in:

```
Dim x As Long
Dim y As Long
Dim z As Long
Dim w As Long
oVBE.ActiveCodePane.GetSelection x, y, z, w
```

Example: Clearing the Debug Window

One of the most glaring (and trivial) omissions to the VB object model is a Clear method for the Debug object. How nice it would be to be able to clear the Immediate window of old text before issuing a **Debug.Print** statement.

Although there is nothing we can do to supply a Clear method for the Debug object, we can at least create a simple add-in that makes it easier to clear the

Immediate window from design mode. The code in Example 7-3, which can be placed in a menu item's Click event, does the trick.

Example 7-3. Code to Clear the Immediate Window

```
Dim winActive As VBIDE.Window
Dim winImm As VBIDE.Window

Set winImm = gVBInst.Windows("Immediate")
If winImm Is Nothing Then Exit Sub

' Save the currently active window
Set winActive = gVBInst.ActiveWindow

'Do not clear if Window Not Visible
If winImm.Visible = True Then
  winImm.SetFocus
  SendKeys "^({Home})", True
  SendKeys "^(+({End}))", True
  SendKeys "{Del}", True
End If

' Return to active window
winActive.SetFocus
Set winImm = Nothing
```

Note that this code uses **SendKeys** statements to clear the Immediate window. Therefore, it must be tested as a compiled DLL so it will run in-process.

Example: Scrolling a Code Pane

The TopLine property is all we need to build a simple scrolling feature that scrolls a code pane. The steps are as follows:

1. Add a new form to your add-in, say *frmScroll*. Here's the code for this form:

```
Private Sub Form_Activate()
   ' Set form dimensions to be out of the way
   Me.Top = 0
   Me.Left = 0
   Me.Width = 5000
   Me.Height = 10
End Sub

Private Sub Form_KeyDown(KeyCode As Integer, _
   Shift As Integer)

   Select Case KeyCode
   Case vbKeyEscape
      bStopScrolling = True
   Case vbKeyUp
      ' Subtract 0.02 to delay rate
```

```
            rDelayRate = rDelayRate - 0.02
            ' Validate
            If rDelayRate <= 0.02 Then
               rDelayRate = 0.02
               Beep
            End If
        Case vbKeyDown
            ' Add 0.02 to delay rate
            rDelayRate = rDelayRate + 0.02
        End Select

        Me.Caption = "Scrolling ... " & rDelayRate

    End Sub

    Private Sub Form_Load()
        Me.KeyPreview = True
        Me.Caption = "Scrolling ... " & rDelayRate
    End Sub
```

2. In the **basMain** standard module, add the following two public declarations:

```
Public bStopScrolling As Boolean
Public rDelayRate As Single
```

Also, add the *Delay* procedure shown in this code snippet:

```
Sub Delay(rTime As Single)

'Delay rTime seconds (min=.01, max=300)

Dim OldTime As Variant

'Safty net
If rTime < 0.01 Or rTime > 300 Then rTime = 1

OldTime = Timer

Do
    DoEvents
Loop Until Timer - OldTime >= rTime

End Sub
```

3. In the Click event for cbcFeature1, add a call to *ScrollCodePane*, and then the *ScrollCodePane* procedure (shown in the following code) to the Connect class module:

```
Sub ScrollCodePane()

Dim lPrevLine As Long
Dim lSafe As Long

rDelayRate = 0.1
frmScroll.Show
```

```
oVBE.ActiveCodePane.TopLine = 1

lSafe = 0
lPrevLine = -1
Do

   lSafe = lSafe + 1

   ' Check for Escape key
   If bStopScrolling Then
      bStopScrolling = False
      Exit Do
   End If

   ' Save this to check for end of code pane
   lPrevLine = oVBE.ActiveCodePane.TopLine

   ' Scroll one line
   oVBE.ActiveCodePane.TopLine = _
      oVBE.ActiveCodePane.TopLine + 1

   ' If no more lines, get out
   If oVBE.ActiveCodePane.TopLine = lPrevLine _
      Then Exit Do

   ' Wait
   Delay rDelayRate

Loop Until lSafe > 10000

Unload frmScroll

End Sub
```

Note that we can increase or decrease scrolling speed using the up and down
arrow keys and stop scrolling by hitting the Esc key.

In this chapter:
• *VB Projects*
• *The VBProjects*
  Collection
• *The VBProject Object*
• *Example: Setting the*
  Start Project

Project-Related Objects

In this chapter, we take a look at the objects that can control Visual Basic projects. Figure 8-1 shows the portions of the VB IDE object model that relates to projects.

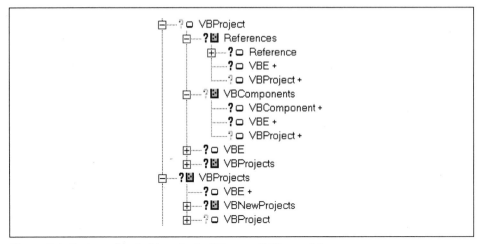

```
┌─── ? □ VBProject
     ├─── ? ▣ References
     │    ├─ ? □ Reference
     │    ├─ ? □ VBE +
     │    └─ ? □ VBProject +
     ├─── ? ▣ VBComponents
     │    ├─ ? □ VBComponent +
     │    ├─ ? □ VBE +
     │    └─ ? □ VBProject +
     ├─── ? □ VBE
     └─── ? ▣ VBProjects
┌─── ? ▣ VBProjects
     ├─ ? □ VBE +
     ├─── ? ▣ VBNewProjects
     └─── ? □ VBProject
```

Figure 8-1. Project-related objects in the VB extensibility model

VB Projects

A *project* is simply a set of modules. A VBProject object represents a project. The currently open projects in an instance of the VB IDE are contained in the VBProjects collection. In other words, a VBProjects collection represents a Visual Basic project *group*. To access this collection, we can use the VBProjects property of the VBE object.

There are two ways to access VBProject objects. The ActiveVBProject property of the VBE object returns the active VBProject object, and the Item method of the VBProjects collection returns an individual VBProject object. For instance, the following line:

```
MsgBox oVBE.VBProjects("AProject").IsDirty
```

indicates whether or not the project named *AProject* has been changed since it was last saved.

The VBProjects Collection

The following list shows the members of the VBProjects collection. We will look at some of the more interesting of these members.

Add	IconState	SaveAs
AddFromFile	Item	StartProject
AddFromTemplate	NewEnum	VBE
Count	Parent	
FileName	Remove	

The FileName property

The FileName property returns the complete path and filename of the VB group file (extension *.vbg*). If the group contains only a single project, there is no *.vbg* file, and the property returns the filename *Group1.vbg* (along with the path to the project files).

The StartProject property

The StartProject property sets or returns the VBProject object that represents the *start project*; that is, the project that executes when the user selects Start from the Run menu. We will see an example that uses this property later in the chapter.

The SaveAs method

This method saves the project group under a given name. Its syntax is:

```
VBProjectsGroup.SaveAs (newfilename As String)
```

where *newfilename* is the new group filename and optional path. (If the path is omitted, the previous path is used.)

Note the following:

— The SaveAs method saves only the *.vbg* file, not the rest of the group files.

— On the other hand, individual VBProject and VBComponent objects have their own SaveAs method, so it's possible to save all of a group's files.

— There is no Save method, but the same effect is achieved using SaveAs with the original filename.

— SaveAs doesn't prompt for replacement of the current version of the *.vbg* file.

The Add and Remove methods

To create a new project and add it to the current project group, use the Add method, whose syntax is:

```
VBProjectsObject.Add( projecttype As vbext_ProjectType, _
    [exclusive As Boolean]) As VBProject
```

The *projecttype* parameter is set to one of the constants in the following enum:

```
Enum vbext_ProjectType
    vbext_pt_StandardExe = 0
    vbext_pt_ActiveXExe = 1
    vbext_pt_ActiveXDll = 2
    vbext_pt_ActiveXControl = 3
End Enum
```

The *exclusive* parameter should be set to **True** to start a new project group and add the new project, which would then be the only project in the group. Set the parameter to **False** (which is the default) to add the new project to the current project group (represented by *VBProjectsObject*). It's important to note that, when *exclusive* is **True**, the Add method replaces the current project group with the new one without confirming any changes.

Add methods typically return the object added, and this Add method is no exception. This makes it easy to manipulate the object immediately after adding it. For instance, to add a new project named *Aproject* to the current project group, we can write:

```
Dim vbp As VBProject
Set vbp = oVBE.VBProjects.Add(vbext_pt_StandardEXE)
vbp.Name = "Aproject"
```

The Remove method removes a project from the project group. For instance, to remove the second project from the group, write:

```
oVBE.VBProjects.Remove(2)
```

But because removing one project changes the indices of the other projects in a group, it's dangerous to refer to a project by index. It's better to remove projects by name, as in:

```
oVBE.VBProjects.Remove("ObjectBrowser")
```

The VBNewProjects Collection

The VB IDE provides a VBNewProjects collection that is returned by the AddFrom-File and AddFromTemplate methods of the VBProjects collection. Each of these methods adds one or more projects to a new or existing group. When the group already has some projects, it may be important to manipulate only the newly added projects. The VBNewProjects collection contains just these projects.

Note that the only way to get a VBNewProjects collection is as the return value of either AddFromFile or AddFromTemplate. Thus, the collection has a temporary nature, in the sense that when a new VB IDE session is started, there is no VBNewProjects collection.

The AddFromFile method

The syntax for the AddFromFile method is:

```
VBProjectsObject.AddFromFile( ByVal pathname As String, _
    [exclusive As Boolean]) As VBNewProjects
```

Here **pathname** is the path and filename of the group file from which to get the new projects to add or replace the current ones. If **exclusive** is `False` (the default), the new projects are added to the current group. If **exclusive** is `True`, the new projects replace the current ones, and the current ones are saved without confirmation.

The AddFromTemplate method

The syntax of the AddFromTemplate method is:

```
VBProjectsObject.AddFromTemplate( ByVal pathname As String, _
    [exclusive As Boolean]) As VBNewProjects
```

The AddFromTemplate method is analogous to the AddFromFile method, the only difference being that the source of the projects to add is from a template (identified by **pathname**) rather than existing project files.

The VBProject Object

As I have said, a VBProject object represents an individual project. The properties and methods of the VBProject object are shown in the following list:

AddToolboxProgID	HelpFile	SaveAs
BuildFileName	IconState	Saved
Collection	IsDirty	StartMode
CompatibleOleServer	MakeCompiledFile	Type
Description	Name	VBComponents
FileName	ReadProperty	VBE
HelpContextID	References	WriteProperty

Let's look at some of these members:

The AddToolboxProgID method

This method is the programmatic version of adding a component to the Toolbox through the Components menu item on the Project menu. The syntax is:

```
VBProjectObject.AddToolboxProgID( ByVal progid As String, _
                    [filename As String])
```

where *progid* is the ProgID for the control that we want to add to the toolbox, and *filename* is an optional string giving the location of a type library. (Type libraries embedded in the *.ocx* file are automatically referenced, so this argument is unnecessary.)

To illustrate, some time ago I wrote a custom volume control that controls the speaker volume. Here is the code that adds this control to the VB toolbox:

```
oVBE.ActiveVBProject.AddToolboxProgID _
   "RPVolumeControl.Ctrl"
```

The BuildFileName property and the MakeCompiledFile method

The BuildFileName property returns or sets the name of the file that will be built when the user chooses the Make option from the File menu.

The MakeCompiledFile method causes the file mentioned above to be built.

The Description, FileName, and Name properties

The Description property reads or sets the project's description. This is the entry in the Project Properties dialog box.

The FileName property returns the complete path and filename of the project, which, of course, isn't the same as the project's name. If the project has not yet been saved, this method returns an empty string.

The Name property of a VBProject object returns the name of the project.

The IsDirty and the Saved properties

The IsDirty property returns or sets a Boolean value indicating whether the project was edited since the last time it was saved. Note that this property is read-write.

The Saved property gives the same information, but it's read-only. (Note that the help documentation discusses what happens if we set this property to **True**, which is very hard to do with a read-only property.)

There is a subtlety here we should try to clarify; namely, that both of these properties are set by the SaveAs method. However, all file components in the project must be saved (and not just the project file) before the properties are changed. For instance, if we have a project file named *Project1.vbp* with a form whose filename is *Form1.frm*, then the code:

```
oVBE.ActiveVBProject.SaveAs "d:\temp\project1.vbp"
```

```
oVBE.ActiveVBProject.VBComponents("Form1").SaveAs _
   "d:\temp\Form1.frm"
```

saves both files and causes the IsDirty and Saved properties to be set correctly. (IsDirty is set to **False** and Saved is set to **True**.)

Now, if we then make a change to the form only, the two properties are reset to IsDirty = **True** and Saved = **False**. However, the code:

```
oVBE.ActiveVBProject.SaveAs "d:\temp\project1.vbp"
```

doesn't change these flags, since the form is still dirty, but the subsequent code:

```
oVBE.ActiveVBProject.VBComponents("Form1").SaveAs _
    "d:\temp\Form1.frm"
```

causes the IsDirty and Saved flags to be changed (and rightly so).

Put another way, the SaveAs method, when applied to a VBProject object, saves only the *.vbp* file. However, the Saved and IsDirty properties of the VBProject object reflect the status of the entire project; that is, of all its files.

The ReadProperty and WriteProperty methods

These two methods are used to read and write a **Key=Value** string from a section in the project's *.vbp*. However, these methods aren't well documented and probably should be avoided. (Is there really a good reason to write to a *.vbp* file?)

The StartMode property

As you may know, the StartMode property determines how an ActiveX EXE project is started when the user starts the project. There are two possible settings in the project's properties dialog: Standalone (Sub Main runs when the user starts the application) or ActiveX component (Sub Main runs only when a client first creates an object).

Accordingly, the StartMode property of the VBProject object can be set to either of the constants in the following enum:

```
Enum vbext_ProjectStartMode
    vbext_psm_StandAlone = 0
    vbext_psm_OleServer = 1
End Enum
```

The VBComponents property

The VBComponents property returns the VBComponents collection of VBComponent objects. We discuss VBComponent objects later in this chapter.

The References Property and Reference Objects

A Reference object represents a reference to a type library (object library). The References property returns the References collection of all Reference objects for the project.

The properties and methods of the Reference object are shown in this list:

BuiltIn	Guid	Name
Collection	IsBroken	Type
Description	Major	VBE
FullPath	Minor	

Here are some of these members:

The BuiltIn property

This read-only property returns a Boolean value indicating whether or not the reference is a default reference and therefore can't be removed. These latter include the references to Visual Basic for Applications, Visual Basic, and the Visual Basic runtime.

The FullPath property

This read-only property returns the path and filename of the referenced type library.

The IsBroken property

This read-only property returns a Boolean value that indicates whether or not the Reference object refers to a type library whose registry entry is valid. If IsBroken is **True**, the reference isn't valid.

The Major and Minor properties

These properties return Long integers that contain the major and minor version number of the referenced type library.

The Name and Description properties

The read-only Name property returns the name of the type library. The read-only Description property returns a description for the type library. This is the text that the References dialog displays when the user selects the References item from the Project menu.

To illustrate, the following code:

```
For Each ref In oVBE.ActiveVBProject.References
    Debug.Print ref.Description & "/" & ref.Name
Next
```

produces the following output on one particular project:

```
Visual Basic For Applications/VBA
Visual Basic runtime objects and procedures/VBRUN
Visual Basic objects and procedures/VB
OLE Automation/stdole
Desaware SpyWorks 5.0 VB Subclasser/dwSpyVB
Microsoft DAO 3.5 Object Library/DAO
Microsoft Visual Basic 5.0 Extensibility/VBIDE
Microsoft Word 8.0 Object Library/Word
```

The References Collection

The AddFromFile method of the References collection can add a reference to the References collection for a project:

```
ReferencesCollection.AddFromFile(filename)
```

where *filename* is the name of the file that we wish to reference. Note that the AddFromFile method returns the Reference object that is added to the References collection. For example, to add a reference to the Word 8 Object Model (filename *msword8.olb*) we would write:

```
oVBE.ActiveVBProject.References.AddFromFile _
    "i:\office97\office\msword8.olb"
```

(here *i:\office97\office* is the path to this reference on my PC).

To refer to a specific reference, we can use the Item method with either the usual index parameter of the reference (one-based) or else the name of the reference. Unfortunately, we need to do a little preliminary experimenting (by adding the reference and then checking its Name property) to determine the correct name. For instance, the Word reference added above has the name Word, as in the following code:

```
aiMsg.AddItem oVBE.ActiveVBProject.References("Word").GUID
```

The References collection also has a Remove method for removing references:

```
ReferencesCollection.Remove(ReferenceObject)
```

where *ReferenceObject* refers to a Reference object. For instance, the following line removes the reference to Word:

```
With oVBE.ActiveVBProject
    References.Remove .References("Word")
End With
```

Note that we can also add a reference using the AddFromGUID method, but this requires knowledge of the GUID, and the major and minor version numbers, of the type library.

The VBComponent Object

A VBComponent object represents a component in a VB project. The read-only Type property of the VBComponent object reveals what kind of component the object represents. This property can assume any value in the following enum:

```
Enum vbext_ComponentType
    vbext_ct_StdModule = 1
    vbext_ct_ClassModule = 2
    vbext_ct_MSForm = 3
    vbext_ct_ResFile = 4
```

```
        vbext_ct_VBForm = 5
        vbext_ct_VBMDIForm = 6
        vbext_ct_PropPage = 7
        vbext_ct_UserControl = 8
        vbext_ct_DocObject = 9
        vbext_ct_RelatedDocument = 10
        vbext_ct_ActiveXDesigner = 11
    End Enum
```

The properties and methods of the VBComponent object are shown in this list:

Activate	FileNames	ReadProperty
CodeModule	HasOpenDesigner	Reload
Collection	HelpContextID	SaveAs
Description	IconState	Type
Designer	InsertFile	VBE
DesignerID	IsDirty	WriteProperty
DesignerWindow	Name	
FileCount	Properties	

The following properties and methods merit further attention:

The Activate method

This method causes the component to be activated. It has the same effect as if the user double-clicked on this item in the Project window. Note that the Activate method doesn't activate the code behind a form (but it does activate the form).

The CodeModule property

This read-only property returns a CodeModule object, which represents the code behind the component. We discuss CodeModule objects in Chapter 11, *Code-Related Objects*. Note that if the component doesn't have a code module associated with it, this property returns Nothing.

It's important to make a clear distinction between a CodePane object and a CodeModule object. A CodePane object displays the code in a code module. Indeed, there can be several CodePanes in a single VB component, but only one CodeModule.

The Description property

This property can set or read the description of the component. Recall that to set the description of a component using the user interface, we need to use Microsoft's Object Browser, as described earlier in our discussion of creating the Connect class.

The FileCount and FileNames properties

The read-only FileCount property returns the number of files associated with a given component. The primary use (perhaps the only use) for this property is to determine whether or not a component of type **vbext_ct_VBForm** has an associated *.frx* file (which contains nontext data for the form), in which case the FileCount property returns 2 instead of 1.

The FileNames property returns the current path and filename(s) for the component. The syntax is:

```
VBComponentObject.FileNames(Index)
```

where *Index* can be any Long from 1 to *FileCount*. Thus, *Index* should be set to 1 except when there is an *.frx* file for a form, in which case we can get this path by setting *Index* equal to 2.

Note that the path returned is always a complete (absolute) path, even if the value in the *vbp* file is a relative path.

The IsDirty property

The IsDirty property applies both to the VBComponent object and the VBProject object. See the discussion of this property for the VBProject object.

The Name property

This property returns or sets the name used in code to identify an object (not the component's filename).

The Properties collection

The Properties property of a VBComponent object returns a Properties collection. This collection contains one Property object for each property of the component. These are the properties that appear in the Properties window.

To illustrate, the following code:

```
On Error Resume Next
Dim p As Property
For Each p In oVBE.ActiveVBProject.VBComponents(1).Properties
    Debug.Print p.Name & " = " & p.Value
Next
```

produces the list shown in Example 8-1 for a component of type **vbext_ct_VBForm** (the list has been sorted).

Example 8-1. Properties of a Component of Type vbext_ct_VBForm

```
Appearance = 1
AutoRedraw = False
BackColor = -2147483633
BorderStyle = 2
Caption = Form1
ClipControls = True
ControlBox = True
DrawMode = 13
DrawStyle = 0
DrawWidth = 1
Enabled = True
FillColor = 0
```

Example 8-1. Properties of a Component of Type vbext_ct_VBForm (continued)

```
FillStyle = 1
FontTransparent = True
ForeColor = -2147483630
HasDC = True (VB6 only)
Height = 2880
HelpContextID = 0
KeyPreview = False
Left = 0
LinkMode = 0
LinkTopic = Form1
MaxButton = True
MDIChild = False
MinButton = True
MousePointer = 0
Moveable = True
Name = Form1
NegotiateMenus = True
OLEDropMode = 0
PaletteMode = 0
RightToLeft = False
ScaleHeight = 2364
ScaleLeft = 0
ScaleMode = 1
ScaleTop = 0
ScaleWidth = 3672
ShowInTaskbar = True
StartUpPosition = 3
Tag =
Top = 0
Visible = True
WhatsThisButton = False
WhatsThisHelp = False
Width = 3840
WindowState = 0
```

Note that the Font, Icon, MouseIcon, Palette, and Picture properties don't have values. Attempting to access this value produces an error (which is why we included the On Error line).

The Reload method

The Reload method reloads the component from the disk file, thereby discarding any unsaved changes. The Reload method causes the IsDirty property to be set to **False**.

The SaveAs method

This method saves the component as the specified filename and sets the IsDirty property to False. Its syntax is:

```
ComponentObject.SaveAs(FileName)
```

where *FileName* is the name of the file to which the component is to be saved. The method returns **True** to indicate success and **False** for failure. To illustrate, the following code saves the first component, overwriting the existing file:

```
oVBE.ActiveVBProject.VBComponents(1).SaveAs _
    oVBE.ActiveVBProject.VBComponents(1).FileNames(1)
```

Note that if the component is a form and there is an accompanying *.frx* file, it is also saved by this code.

The Type property

This read-only property returns the type of component. It can be any of the constants in the following enum:

```
Enum vbext_ComponentType
    vbext_ct_StdModule = 1
    vbext_ct_ClassModule = 2
    vbext_ct_MSForm = 3
    vbext_ct_ResFile = 4
    vbext_ct_VBForm = 5
    vbext_ct_VBMDIForm = 6
    vbext_ct_PropPage = 7
    vbext_ct_UserControl = 8
    vbext_ct_DocObject = 9
    vbext_ct_RelatedDocument = 10
    vbext_ct_ActiveXDesigner = 11
End Enum
```

Designers

The VBComponent objects of the following types:

- vbext_ct_VBForm
- vbext_ct_DocObject
- vbext_ct_UserControl

require a special container to assist in the design of the component (adding controls, for instance). This container is called a *designer*.

Microsoft has not seen fit to document designers very well, but it appears that there is no such thing as a Designer object per se. This is reinforced by the fact that the VBIDE object library doesn't contain a Designer object.

Let's do some investigating. First, we create a client project with one form, one UserControl, and one UserDocument. Then we place the code shown in Example 8-2 in one of the Click events of our add-in shell. This code cycles through each component in the client project. For each component, it displays the component's name and type, as well as the ProgID of the component's designer "object." The results are shown in Figure 8-2. Then, as a test, the code sets the return value of the Designer property to a variable of type VBForm.

Example 8-2. Code to Investigate Designers

```
Dim vbc As VBComponent
Dim vbf As VBForm
Dim vbctl As VBControl

For Each vbc In oVBE.ActiveVBProject.VBComponents

    aiMsg.AddItem vbc.Name & "/" & vbc.Type & _
        "/" & vbc.DesignerID
    Set vbf = vbc.Designer
    Set vbctl = vbf.VBControls.Add("VB.TextBox")

Next
```

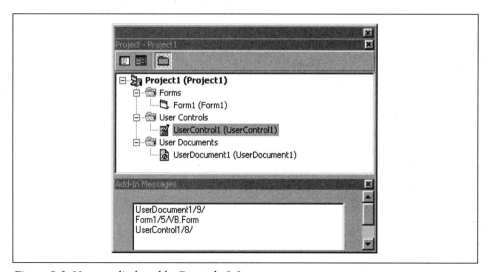

Figure 8-2. Message displayed by Example 8-2

Now, it appears from the fact that this code runs without error that VB is happy with the assignment of the Designer property to a variable of type VBForm in all three cases; that is, each designer appears to be an object of type VBForm. However, the output in Figure 8-2 shows that the Designer for the form is the only one that has a ProgID equal to VBForm.

In any case, it doesn't seem to matter, for we can just manipulate the designer "object" as though it was an object of type VBForm. In fact, Example 8-2 creates a new text box on each component!

You should note the following facts about designers:

- If a component doesn't have an associated designer, the Designer property returns Nothing. This is true for standard and class modules, for instance.

- Each designer resides in a window. The associated Window object is returned by the DesignerWindow property of the component. Accessing the Designer-Window property of a component creates the designer, but doesn't make it visible. To make the window visible, set the Window object's Visible property to True.

- We can check to see if a particular component's designer is open (assuming it has a designer) by using the HasOpenDesigner Boolean property.

We discuss VBForm objects in Chapter 9, *Form and Control Objects*, but let's now observe that this discussion emphasizes that a VBComponent object of type vbext_ct_VBForm isn't the same as a (designer) object of type VBForm.

The VBComponents Collection

The VBComponents property of the VBProject object returns a VBComponents collection that contains the VBComponent objects for that project. The properties and methods of the VBComponents collection are given in the following list:

Add	Count	Remove
AddCustom	Item	StartUpObject
AddFile	NewEnum	VBE
AddFromTemplate	Parent	

Here are some of these members:

The Add and Remove methods

The Add method adds a new component to a project. The syntax is:

```
VBComponentsCollection.Add(componenttype)
```

where **componenttype** is one of the following **vbext_ComponentType** constants:

```
vbext_ct_StdModule = 1
vbext_ct_ClassModule = 2
vbext_ct_VBForm = 5
vbext_ct_VBMDIForm = 6
vbext_ct_PropPage = 7
vbext_ct_UserControl = 8
vbext_ct_DocObject = 9
```

(Of course, the project must be willing to accept a component of the chosen type.) Note that the following constants aren't allowed:

```
vbext_ct_MSForm = 3
vbext_ct_ResFile = 4
vbext_ct_RelatedDocument = 10
vbext_ct_ActiveXDesigner = 11
```

and produce a nasty error message, as shown in Figure 8-3.

Figure 8-3. Error when adding an unsupported component to the VBComponents collection

As usual, the Add method returns the VBComponent object that it creates, making it easy to manipulate the object immediately after adding it.

The Remove method removes a component from the project. Its syntax is:

```
VBComponentsObject.Remove(VBComponentObject)
```

For instance, the following code removes the component named *Class1*:

```
oVBE.ActiveVBProject.VBComponents.Remove _
oVBE.ActiveVBProject.VBComponents("Class1")
```

The AddFile method

The AddFile method creates a new component from an existing file. The syntax is:

```
VBComponentsObject.AddFile (pathname, relateddocument)
```

where *pathname* is the complete path and filename of the file, and *relateddocument* is an optional Boolean value that is set to **True** to add the file as a related file (whatever that is) and **False** (the default) to add the file as a VB component.

Note that files that are normally VB project components, such as form files, cause an error if the *relateddocument* parameter is set to **True**. Indeed, the *relateddocument* parameter is required only when adding text files that can be treated as either standard modules or as related documents (and we want the file to be treated as a related document).

The AddFromTemplate method

This method, whose syntax is:

```
VBComponentsObject.AddFromTemplate(pathname)
```

where *pathname* is the complete path and filename of a VB template file, creates a new VB component based on the template, just as though the user selected an icon from one of the Add dialog boxes. For instance, the following line creates a new "Tip of the Day" form:

```
oVBE.ActiveVBProject.VBComponents.AddFromTemplate _
    "H:\VB5\Template\Forms\Tip of the Day.frm"
```

The StartupObject property

This property sets the startup object in the project. Its syntax is:

```
VBComponents.StartupObject = startupconstant
```

where **startupconstant** is one of the constants in the following enum:

```
Enum vbext_StartupObject
    vbext_so_SubMain = 0
    vbext_so_None = 1
End Enum
```

These choices correspond to the choices in the Startup Object drop-down box in the Properties dialog box.

Example: Setting the Start Project

Using the StartProject property, we can easily create an add-in feature that displays the current projects and allows the user to change this project with a single keystroke (assuming that there are at most nine projects in the group). The steps to create this add-in are as follows:

1. Add a global integer variable to the **basMain** module:

    ```
    Public giStartProject As Integer
    ```

2. Add a form called frmStartProject to the add-in. On this form, place a label called lblProjects that occupies almost the entire form. Here is the code for the form:

    ```
    Private Sub Form_KeyPress(KeyAscii As Integer)

    giStartProject = KeyAscii - 48
    If giStartProject < 1 Or giStartProject > 9 Then _
        giStartProject = 1
    Unload Me

    End Sub


    Private Sub Form_Load()

    Me.Caption = "Set Start Project"
    lblProjects.Font.Name = "Courier New"
    lblProjects.Font.Size = 10

    End Sub
    ```

3. Add a call to the SetStartProject procedure in the Click event as usual. The procedure (which should be placed in the Connect class module) is shown in Figure 8-4. The following is the source code for the SetStartProject procedure:

```
Sub SetStartProject()

Dim sText As String
Dim i As Integer
Dim sPrefix As String

giStartProject = 1
sText = ""

For i = 1 To oVBE.VBProjects.Count
    ' Prefix start project with *
    If oVBE.VBProjects(i) Is _
        oVBE.VBProjects.StartProject Then
        sPrefix = "*"
    Else
        sPrefix = "  "
    End If

    sText = sText & sPrefix & Format$(i) & _
        ": " & oVBE.VBProjects(i).Name & vbCrLf
Next i

frmStartProject.lblProjects = sText
frmStartProject.Show vbModal

oVBE.VBProjects.StartProject = _
oVBE.VBProjects(giStartProject)

End Sub
```

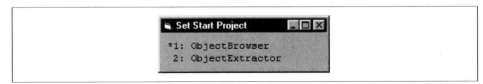

Figure 8-4. The SetStartProject procedure

Now, when the user invokes this feature, the add-in displays the list of current projects in the group, as shown in Figure 8-4. The current start project is marked by an asterisk. If the user hits the number keys 1–9, the form unloads and the chosen project becomes the start project. Any other key just unloads the modal form.

Form and Control Objects

In this chapter, we take a look at the objects that can control Visual Basic forms. Figure 9-1 shows the portions of the VB IDE object model that relate to forms; it's headed by the VBForm object.

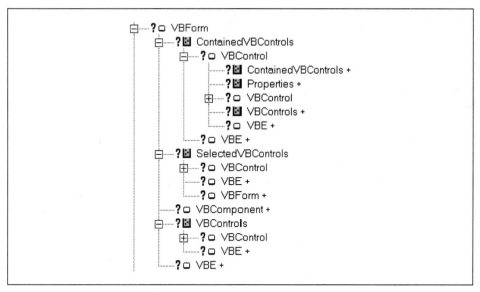

```
?□ VBForm
    ?🖭 ContainedVBControls
        ?□ VBControl
            ?🖭 ContainedVBControls +
            ?🖭 Properties +
            ?□ VBControl
            ?🖭 VBControls +
            ?□ VBE +
        ?□ VBE +
    ?🖭 SelectedVBControls
        ?□ VBControl
        ?□ VBE +
        ?□ VBForm +
    ?□ VBComponent +
    ?🖭 VBControls
        ?□ VBControl
        ?□ VBE +
    ?□ VBE +
```

Figure 9-1. Form and Control objects

The VBForm Object

Let's begin by recalling that a VBForm object isn't the same as a VBComponent object of type **vbext_ct_VBForm**. Indeed, a VBForm object is obtained from the

Designer property of a VBComponent object of type **vbext_ct_VBForm**. For example, the following code:

```
Dim vbf As VBForm

Set vbf = oVBE.ActiveVBProject. _
    VBComponents("Form1").Designer

aiMsg.AddItem  vbf.SelectedVBControls(0). _
    Properties("Name").Value
```

displays the name of the first selected control on the VBForm object associated with the form named *Form1.*

Although it's technically inaccurate, if *vbf* refers to a VBForm object, we will use the phrase "the form *vbf*" instead of the more clumsy phrase "the form associated with the *vbf* designer."

The previous code illustrates some interesting points about VBControl objects:

- The SelectedVBControls collection is 0-based
- A VBControl object doesn't have a Name property

The members of the VBForm object are shown in the following list:

CanPaste	Paste	VBControls
ContainedVBControls	SelectAll	VBE
Parent	SelectedVBControls	

The SelectAll method

The SelectAll method selects all controls on the given form.

The Paste method and the CanPaste property

If the Clipboard currently contains an item that can be pasted on a form, the read-only CanPaste property is **True**. In this event, we can invoke the Paste method to paste that item onto the form.

VBControls Collections

The VBForm object has three properties that return collections of controls:

- The VBControl property
- The SelectedVBControls property
- The ContainedVBControls property

As expected, the VBControls collection is the collection of all controls on the form, and the SelectedVBControls collection is the collection of all currently selected controls.

To understand the ContainedVBControls collection, we must understand that every control is contained in a component called its *container*. When a control is placed directly on a form, the form becomes the control's container. Some controls, such as frames and picture boxes, can act as containers for other controls. The ContainedVBControls collection is the collection of all controls whose container is the form. As we will see, controls also have a ContainedVBControls collection.

The properties and methods of the VBControls and ContainedVBControls collections are identical and are shown in the following list:

Add	NewEnum	VBE
Count	Parent	
Item	Remove	

The members of the SelectedVBControls collection are different, as we would expect (see the following list), since selected controls can be cut, copied, and cleared, and we can't "add" or "remove" a control from this collection.

Clear	Cut	Parent
Copy	Item	VBE
Count	NewEnum	

The Add method

The only method that needs commenting on in the previous two lists is the Add method, which adds a control to the VBControls or ContainedVBControls collection. The syntax is:

```
object.Add(progid, relativevbcontrol, before)
```

where *object* is a reference to either a VBControls or a ContainedVBControls collection.

The *progid* parameter is a string that gives the ProgID of the control to add. It has the form *VB.controlname*. The following list gives the ProgIDs for the most common VB controls:

VB.CheckBox	VB.Frame	VB.OptionButton
VB.ComboBox	VB.HScrollBar	VB.PictureBox
VB.CommandButton	VB.Image	VB.Shape
VB.Control	VB.Label	VB.TextBox
VB.DirListBox	VB.Line	VB.Timer
VB.DriveListBox	VB.ListBox	VB.VscrollBar
VB.FileListBox	VB.OLE	

The optional *relativevbcontrol* is of type VBControl and, according to Microsoft, somehow specifies the location at which the new component is to be placed. (It doesn't seem to do anything on my system.) The optional Boolean parameter *before* specifies whether the new control is placed before or after the *relativevbcontrol* control.

The VBControl Object

The VBControl object represents a VB control. VBControl objects are contained in the three VB controls collection that we discussed above. The properties and methods of a VBControl object are shown in the following list:

ClassName	ControlObject	Properties
Collection	ControlType	VBE
ContainedVBControls	InSelection	WizardHook
Container	ProgId	ZOrder

The ProgId and ClassName properties

The ProgID property returns the programmatic ID of the control, and the ClassName property returns the class name for the control. The class name is the name to the right of the period in the programmatic ID, as shown in the last list in the previous section.

The ContainedVBControls property

As discussed earlier, this property returns the ContainedVBControls collection that represents all VBControl objects whose container is the given control. If the control isn't a container, ContainedVBControls is an empty collection. (We *might* have expected the ContainedVBControls property to return **Nothing**.)

The Container property

To return or set the container for a control, use the *Container* property. For instance, the code:

```
Dim vbf As VBForm

Set vbf = oVBE.ActiveVBProject. _
    VBComponents("Form1").Designer

Set vbf.VBControls("Text1").Container = _
    vbf.VBControls("Frame1")
```

places the control named Text1 inside the control named Frame1. Similarly, the code:

```
Dim vbf As VBForm

Set vbf = oVBE.ActiveVBProject. _
    VBComponents("Form1").Designer

Set vbf.VBControls("Text1").Container = vbf
```

moves the Text1 control back to the form.

Experimentation indicates that after executing these procedures, the user may have some trouble moving the controls with the mouse. However, setting the Top and Left properties immediately after the previous code seems to resolve the problem.

The ControlType property

This read-only property returns the type of the control and can be one of the constants in the following enum:

```
Enum vbext_ControlType
    vbext_ct_Light = 1
    vbext_ct_Standard = 2
    vbext_ct_Container = 3
End Enum
```

Note that a *light* control has no *hWnd* window handle, a *standard* control has an *hWnd,* and a *container* control can act as a container.

The InSelection property

This Boolean property can be set to **True** to select the control or **False** to deselect the control. Note that if we select a control that is contained within a container control, then all controls that aren't in that container will be deselected.

The Properties property

The Properties property returns the Properties collection for a control. As with the VBComponent object, this collection contains one Property object for each property of the control. These are the properties that appear in the Properties window.

To illustrate, the following code prints the properties and their values for a textbox control:

```
Dim vbf As VBForm
Dim p As Property

On Error Resume Next

Set vbf = oVBE.ActiveVBProject. _
    VBComponents("Form1").Designer

For Each p In vbf.VBControls("Text1").Properties
    Debug.Print p.Name & " = " & p.Value
Next
```

The ZOrder method

This method brings a control to the front of the ZOrder or sends it to the back. In particular, the code:

```
VBControlObject.ZOrder 0
```

moves the control to the front, and:

```
VBControlObject.ZOrder 1
```
sends it to the back. We can also use the more intuitive constants from the VB enum:

```
Enum ZOrderConstants
    vbBringToFront = 0
    vbSendToBack = 1
End Enum
```

Example: Setting Tab Stops

As you may know, VB comes with an example add-in that can set the tab stops for all controls on a form at one time. This example is fairly sophisticated. It uses a ToolWindow and even keeps track of changes to the controls (additions and deletions) on the current form. Let's construct a simpler version of this add-in, modeled in part after the VB5 example.

Our version simply displays a modal form with a list of the controls on the current form, as shown in Figure 9-2. The list box shows each control's tab index, followed by its name, array index (if it has one), and caption (if it has one). The Up and Down buttons move the selected control up or down in the list. The SetTabIndex button sets the control's tab indices according to the new list order and then refreshes the list. Note that the form's caption contains the caption of the selected form (to which the list applies).

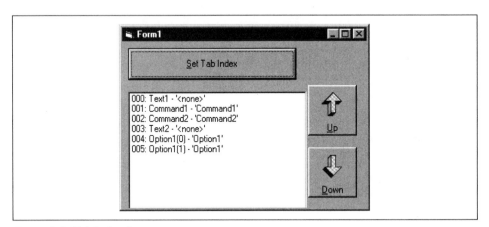

Figure 9-2. Tab Index form

The controls needed to create the form shown in Figure 9-2, as well as their non-default properties, are shown in Table 9-1. The code for this form appears in Example 9-1. To use this set tab index feature, just add a `frmSetTabIndex.Show vbModal` call in a menu item in the add-in shell.

Table 9-1. Tab Index Form Controls and Their Nondefault Properties

Control	Property	Value
Form	Name	frmSetTabIndex
CommandButton	Name	cmdSetTabIndex
	Caption	&Set Tab Index
CommandButton	Name	cmdUp
	Caption	&Up
	Style	1 – Graphical
	Picture	...\Graphics\Icons\Arrows\ Arw06up.ico
CommandButton	Name	cmdDown
	Caption	&Down
	Style	1 – Graphical
	Picture	...\Graphics\Icons\Arrows\ Arw06dn.ico
ListBox	Name	lstTabs
	Sorted	True

Example 9-1. Code for the Tab Index Form

```
Option Explicit

Private cmpCurrent As VBComponent

'-----
Private Sub cmdDown_Click()
On Error Resume Next
  Dim iItem As Integer
  With lstTabs
    If .ListIndex < 0 Then Exit Sub
    iItem = .ListIndex
    ' Cannot move last item down
    If iItem = .ListCount - 1 Then Exit Sub
    ' Move item down one
    .AddItem .Text, iItem + 2
    ' Remove old item
    .RemoveItem iItem
    ' Select the item again
    .Selected(iItem + 1) = True
  End With
  Err.Clear
End Sub

'-----
Private Sub cmdUp_Click()
Dim iItem As Integer
On Error Resume Next
With lstTabs
    If .ListIndex <= 0 Then Exit Sub
    iItem = .ListIndex
    ' Move item up
```

Example 9-1. Code for the Tab Index Form (continued)

```
        .AddItem .Text, iItem - 1
        ' Remove old item
        .RemoveItem iItem + 1
        ' Select the item again
        .Selected(iItem - 1) = True
    End With
    Err.Clear
End Sub

'-----
Private Sub Form_Load()
RefreshList
End Sub
Private Sub Form_Resize()
lstTabs.Width = ScaleWidth - _
    (lstTabs.Left * 2 + cmdUp.Width + 100)
lstTabs.Height = ScaleHeight - _
    (cmdSetTabIndex.Height + 100)
End Sub

'-----
Sub RefreshList()

Dim ctl As VBControl

lstTabs.Clear

'Get selected component
Set cmpCurrent = oVBE.SelectedVBComponent

' Is there a current component?
If cmpCurrent Is Nothing Then Exit Sub

' Is it of correct type?
If (cmpCurrent.Type <> vbext_ct_VBForm) And _
   (cmpCurrent.Type <> vbext_ct_UserControl) And _
   (cmpCurrent.Type <> vbext_ct_DocObject) And _
   (cmpCurrent.Type <> vbext_ct_PropPage) Then
    Exit Sub
End If

' OK to procede
Me.Caption = oVBE.SelectedVBComponent.Name

For Each ctl In cmpCurrent.Designer.VBControls
    lstTabs.AddItem Format$( _
    ctl.Properties!TabIndex, "000") & ": " & _
    ControlDesc(ctl)
Next

End Sub

'-----
Function ControlDesc(ctl As VBIDE.VBControl) As String
```

Example 9-1. Code for the Tab Index Form (continued)

```
' Description of control for list box

On Error Resume Next

Dim sName As String
Dim sCaption As String
Dim i As Integer

sName = ctl.Properties!Name

sCaption = "<none>"
' If there is no caption, then
' error is trapped so sCaption will be <none>
sCaption = ctl.Properties!Caption

i = ctl.Properties!Index
If i >= 0 Then
  sName = sName & "(" & i & ")"
End If

If Len(sCaption) > 0 Then
  ControlDesc = sName & " - '" & sCaption & "'"
Else
  ControlDesc = sName
End If

Err.Clear

End Function

'-----
Private Sub cmdSetTabIndex_Click()

On Error GoTo cmdSetTabIndex_ERROR

Dim i As Integer
Dim sName As String
Dim iCtlArrayIdx As Integer

Screen.MousePointer = vbHourglass

For i = 0 To lstTabs.ListCount - 1

  GetNameAndIndex lstTabs.List(i), _
    sName, iCtlArrayIdx

  If iCtlArrayIdx >= 0 Then
    ' This control is a member of an array
    cmpCurrent.Designer.VBControls.Item( _
      sName, iCtlArrayIdx).Properties!TabIndex = i
  Else
    ' Not part of control array -- no index value
```

Example 9-1. Code for the Tab Index Form (continued)

```
        cmpCurrent.Designer.VBControls.Item(sName). _
          Properties!TabIndex = i
  End If
Next

RefreshList

Screen.MousePointer = vbDefault
Exit Sub

cmdSetTabIndex_ERROR:
  If MsgBox(Err.Description & vbCrLf & _
    "Resume?", vbYesNo) = vbYes Then
    Resume Next
  End If
  Screen.MousePointer = vbDefault
End Sub

'-----
Sub GetNameAndIndex(ByVal sItem As String, ByRef sName As String, ByRef iIndex As
Integer)

' Fills out parameters sName with control's name
' and iIndex with control's index (or -1)
' NOTE: item has form:
'     number: name(index) - 'caption'

Dim x As Integer
Dim sTemp As String

' First trim away number
sTemp = Trim$(Mid$(sItem, InStr(sItem, ":") + 1))

' Look for ( to signal index
x = InStr(sTemp, "(")
If x > 0 Then
   sName = Left$(sTemp, x - 1)
   iIndex = Val(Mid$(sTemp, x + 1))
Else
   ' No index.
   iIndex = -1
   'Name is to left of -
   x = InStr(sTemp, "-")
   If x > 0 Then
      sName = Trim$(Left$(sTemp, x - 1))
   Else
      sName = Trim$(sTemp)
   End If
End If

End Sub
```

10

Event-Related Objects

In this chapter, we take a look at the objects in the VBIDE model that provide access to events.

Simply put, the VB IDE object model has some objects that can gain access to certain events that can take place in the VB IDE. These objects are shown in Figure 10-1.

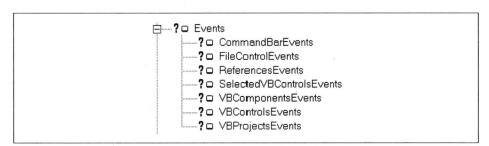

```
⊟──?▢ Events
       ├──?▢ CommandBarEvents
       ├──?▢ FileControlEvents
       ├──?▢ ReferencesEvents
       ├──?▢ SelectedVBControlsEvents
       ├──?▢ VBComponentsEvents
       ├──?▢ VBControlsEvents
       └──?▢ VBProjectsEvents
```

Figure 10-1. VBIDE event objects

The path to these objects is:

```
VBE.Events.ParticularEventObject
```

Put another way, the VBE object has an Events property that returns an Events object. The Events object has seven read-only properties, such as Command-BarEvents, that return a particular event object, such as a CommandBarEvents object.

We have already seen how to use the CommandBarEvents object. In particular, we need only declare a variable of type CommandBarEvents using the `WithEvents` keyword:

```
Private WithEvents CBEventHandler As CommandBarEvents
```

Then we can set this variable to the CommandBarEvents object for the command bar control in question. This is sometimes termed *hooking* the event.

```
Set CBEventHandler = _
    oVBE.Events.CommandBarEvents(cbcThisControl)
```

VB then supplies us with event code shells for the *CBEventHandler* object. Note that, in this case, the CommandBarEvents property takes a single parameter—the command bar control whose events we want to hook—and returns the object associated with that control.

Let's go over the various Events properties and their return values. At the end of this chapter, we discuss code that can experiment with these events.

The CommandBarEvents Object

The syntax for the CommandBarEvents property is:

```
CommandBarEvents(CommandBarControl As Object) _
    As CommandBarEvents
```

We discussed this property and the CommandBarEvents object in Chapter 4, *Menus and Toolbars.*

FileControlEvents

The syntax for the the FileControlEvents property is:

```
FileControlEvents(vbproject As VBProject) _
    As FileControlEvents
```

where *vbproject* is the VBProject object whose file operations we want to hook. Note that setting *vbproject* to `Nothing` hooks file operations for all projects in the project group.

It's worth mentioning that if a project group has more than one project, the FileControlEvents method must be invoked for each project separately if we want to trap all the user's actions with regard to files. For instance, it would be an easy mistake to hook events for the active project:

```
Set XXX = _
oVBE.Events.FileControlEvents(oVBE.ActiveVBProject)
```

and think that the event:

```
Sub XXX_AfterRemoveFile( _
    ByVal VBProject As VBIDE.VBProject, _
    ByVal FileType As VBIDE.vbext_FileType, _
    ByVal FileName As String)
```

will catch any file removed by the user. It won't catch file removals from the non-active project.

Let's now discuss some of the events (that is, methods) that are fired by the File-ControlEvents object. Incidentally, when you are ready to write serious add-ins using these events, we strongly suggest that you to do some experimenting to avoid unexpected results.

The AfterAddFile Event

This event is fired after the user adds an *existing* file (not a new file) to the project using the Add ... items on the Project menu or after the AddFile method of the VBComponent object is invoked.

The syntax for the method is:

```
Sub object_AfterAddFile(vbproject As VBProject, _
    filetype As vbext_FileType, filename As String)
```

where the parameters have the following meaning (and are filled in by VB):

vbproject

   The VBProject object for the project in which the file was added

filetype

   A constant specifying the type of file that was added; the values are from the following enum:

```
Enum vbext_FileType
    vbext_ft_Form = 0
    vbext_ft_Module = 1
    vbext_ft_Class = 2
    vbext_ft_Project = 3
    vbext_ft_Exe = 4
    vbext_ft_Frx = 5
    vbext_ft_Res = 6
    vbext_ft_UserControl = 7
    vbext_ft_PropertyPage = 8
    vbext_ft_DocObject = 9
    vbext_ft_Binary = 10
    vbext_ft_GroupProject = 11
    vbext_ft_Designers = 12
End Enum
```

filename

   The name of the file that was added

The AfterChangeFileName Event

This event occurs after a file in the specified project has been saved for the first time or is saved under a new name. It also occurs when the project is first compiled to an executable file, or when it's compiled to an executable under a new name.

Note that these events may occur as a result of user action or through the SaveAs method of the VBComponent object. However, the MakeCompiledFile method of the VBProject object doesn't trigger the event.

The syntax is:

```
Sub object_AfterChangeFileName ( _
    vbproject As VBProject, _
    filetype As vbext_FileType, _
    newname As String, oldname As String)
```

where the parameters have the following meaning (and are filled in by VB):

vbproject
    The VBProject object for the project in which the file was changed

filetype
    The same as for the AfterAddFile event

newname
    The new name of the file

oldname
    The old name of the file

The AfterCloseFile Event

This event fires after an existing file (project or VB component) is closed or a new file is saved and then closed. The point is that the file must exist on disk for this event to fire.

Note that removing a file doesn't trigger this event. (This is done by the AfterRemoveFile event.) It can only be triggered by choosing New Project from the File menu or by closing VB itself.

Note also that the event fires for each file in the project. Thus, if a project consists of exactly two forms, the event fires three times—once for each form and once for the *.vbp* project file.

The syntax is:

```
Sub object_AfterCloseFile(vbproject As VBProject, _
    filetype As vbext_FileType, _
    filename As String, wasdirty As Boolean)
```

where the parameters are the same as for the previous events, except that the Boolean *wasdirty* reports whether or not changes were saved prior to closing the file. (Thus, for a new file, *wasdirty* is always **False**.)

Finally, we note that the event isn't triggered for *.frx* files.

The AfterRemoveFile Event

This event is fired when a file is removed from the project group. This can be done using the user interface or the Remove method. The syntax is:

```
Sub object_AfterRemoveFile(vbproject As VBProject,_
    filetype As vbext_FileType, filename As String)
```

where the parameters are the same as in the previous events.

As with AfterCloseFile, this event doesn't fire unless there is an existing disk file for the component. In addition, the user can remove files from the nonactive project using the VB menus, and this doesn't trigger the AfterFileRemove event.

The AfterWriteFile Event

This event occurs after a file is written to disk. Its syntax is:

```
Sub object_AfterWriteFile(vbproject As VBProject, _
    filetype As vbext_FileType, filename As String, _
    result As Integer)
```

where the parameters are the same as for the previous events, except that *result* is a constant from the following enum, specifying the results of the write operation:

```
Enum vbextWrite
    vbextWriteSuccess = 0
    vbextWriteCancelled = 1
    vbextWriteFailed = 2
End Enum
```

The BeforeLoadFile Event

This event occurs just before an existing component file is loaded, as when an existing file is added to the project. The event also occurs when an *.frx* file is loaded, as when the user first double-clicks on a form component (assuming it has an associated *.frx* file).

The BeforeLoadFile event is fired prior to the AfterAddFile event (when the latter is fired at all).

The syntax for this event is:

```
Sub object_BeforeLoadFile(vbproject As VBProject, _
    filenames() As String)
```

where the *filenames* array is a String array giving the names of the files to be loaded.

The Other Events

The DoGetNewFileName event occurs whenever a SaveAs operation is begun. The RequestChangeFileName event occurs after specifying a new filename for the file, and the name change is completed. The RequestWriteName event occurs before saving any file.

To illustrate these events, here is the sequence of events when we save a form named *Form1.frm* under the name *Main.frm*:

```
DoGetNewFileName: d:\temp\Form1.frm to d:\temp\Form1.frm
RequestChangeFileName: d:\temp\Form1.frm to d:\temp\Main.frm
RequestWriteName: d:\temp\Main.frm
File written to: d:\temp\Main.frm
File changed: d:\temp\Form1.frm to d:\temp\Main.frm
```

Unfortunately, these events are poorly documented and seem to be unreliable. For instance, we would expect to be able to set the *Cancel* parameter in either the RequestChangeFileName event or the RequestWriteName event to **True** in order to abort the event. However, in the first case, it seems that this has no effect, and in the latter case, the file isn't written to disk, but an apparently untrappable "Unspecified System Error" message is generated. In any case, careful testing is in order before attempting to use these events.

ReferencesEvents

The syntax for the ReferencesEvents property is:

```
ReferencesEvents(vbproject As VBProject) As ReferencesEvents
```

As before, we can set *vbproject* to Nothing to hook references activity for all projects in the project group. There are two References events—ItemAdded and ItemRemoved:

The ItemAdded event
   This event occurs when a reference is added to the project, either by the user or through add-in code, using the AddFromFile method of the References collection. Its syntax is:

```
Sub object_ItemAdded(itemadded As Reference)
```

   where *itemadded* is the Reference object that was added to the project.

The ItemRemoved event
   This event occurs when a reference is removed from the project, through either the user interface or the Remove method of the References collection. Its syntax is:

```
Sub object_ItemRemoved(item As Reference)
```

where *item* is the Reference object that was removed from the project.

SelectedVBControlsEvents

The syntax for the SelectedVBControlsEvents property is:

```
SelectedVBControlsEvents(vbproject As VBProject, _
    vbform As VBForm) As SelectedVBControlsEvents
```

where *vbproject* is the project, and *vbform* is the VBForm object whose selected control events we wish to hook. To hook the events for all of the selected controls in a project, we can set *vbform* to Nothing. To hook all projects in the project group, we can also set *vbproject* to Nothing.

There are two SelectedVBControls events—ItemAdded and ItemRemoved:

The ItemAdded event

This event occurs after a control is added to the SelectedVBControls collection; that is, when a control is selected with the mouse using Shift+Click. The syntax is:

```
Sub object_ItemAdded(vbcontrol As VBControl)
```

where *vbcontrol* is the VBControl object that was selected. (Note that there seems to be an anomaly in connection with this event. Experiments indicate that if a single control is selected, and we select another control with the mouse using Shift+Click, the ItemAdded event is fired twice. Also, the Count property of the SelectedVBControls collection may not be valid within this event. I suggest you check this out carefully before relying on this event.)

The ItemRemoved event

This event occurs when a control is removed from the SelectedVBControls collection; that is, when the control is unselected. Its syntax is:

```
Sub object_ItemRemoved(vbcontrol As VBControl)
```

where *vbcontrol* is the VBControl object that is being unselected.

VBComponentsEvents

The syntax for the VBComponentsEvents property is:

```
VBComponentsEvents(vbproject As VBProject) _
    As VBComponentsEvents
```

As usual, we can set *vbproject* to Nothing to hook component-related events for all projects simultaneously.

The ItemActivated event

This event, with syntax:

```
Sub object_ItemActivated(vbcomponent As VBComponent)
```

is fired when a component is double-clicked in the Project window. Note that it returns (in the out parameter **vbcomponent**) the component that is now active. It's also triggered by the Activate method of the VBComponent object.

The ItemAdded event

This event occurs after a component is added to the current project. The syntax is:

```
Sub object_ItemAdded(vbcomponent As VBComponent)
```

where **vbcomponent** is the VBComponent object that was added to the project.

The Reloaded event

This event occurs when the component is reloaded. The syntax is:

```
Sub object_ItemReloaded(vbcomponent As VBComponent)
```

The ItemRemoved event

This event occurs when a component is removed from the project. Its syntax is:

```
Sub object_ItemRemoved(vbcomponent As VBComponent)
```

where **vbcomponent** is the VBComponent object that is being removed.

The ItemRenamed event

This event occurs when a component is renamed (that is, when its Name property is changed, not when its filename is changed). Its syntax is:

```
Sub object_ItemRenamed(vbcomponent As _
    VBComponent, OldName as String)
```

where **vbcomponent** is the VBComponent object that is being renamed, and **OldName** is the original name of the component.

The ItemSelected event

This event occurs when the component is selected by single-clicking on it in the Project window. It also occurs when the Window object containing the code gains the focus. Its syntax is:

```
Sub object_ItemSelected(vbcomponent As VBComponent)
```

VBControlsEvents

The syntax for the VBControlsEvents property is:

```
VBControlsEvents(vbproject As VBProject, _
    vbform As VBForm) As VBControlsEvents
```

where *vbproject* is the project and *vbform* is the VBForm object whose control events we wish to hook. To hook the events for all of the controls in a project, we can set *vbform* to Nothing. To hook all projects in the project group, we can also set *vbproject* to Nothing.

The ItemAdded event

This event occurs after a control is added to *vbform*. The syntax is:

```
Sub object_ItemAdded(vbcontrol As VBControl)
```

where *vbcontrol* is the VBControl object that was added.

The ItemRemoved event

This event occurs when a control is removed from *vbform*. Its syntax is:

```
Sub object_ItemRemoved(vbcontrol As VBControl)
```

where *vbcontrol* is the VBControl object that is being removed.

The ItemRenamed event

This event occurs when a control is renamed. Its syntax is:

```
Sub object_ItemRenamed(vbcontrol As VBControl, _
    oldname As String, oldindex As Long)
```

where *oldindex* is the index of the control or −1 if the control isn't part of a control array.

VBProjectsEvents

The syntax of the VBProjectsEvents property is:

```
VBProjectsEvents() As VBProjectsEvents
```

The ItemActivated event

This event, with syntax:

```
Sub object_ItemActivated(vbproject As VBProject)
```

is fired whenever a component within the project is selected.

The ItemAdded event

This event occurs after a project is added to the project group. The syntax is:

```
Sub object_ItemAdded(vbproject As VBProject)
```

where *vbproject* is the VBProject object that was added.

The Reloaded event

This event occurs when the project is reloaded. The syntax is:

```
Sub object_ItemReloaded(vbproject As VBProject)
```

The ItemRemoved event

This event occurs when a project is removed from the project group. Its syntax is:

```
Sub object_ItemRemoved(vbproject As VBProject)
```

where ***vbproject*** is the VBProject object that is being removed.

The ItemRenamed event

This event occurs when a project is renamed (that is, when its Name property, but not its filename, is changed). Its syntax is:

```
Sub object_ItemRenamed(vbproject As VBProject, _
    OldName As String)
```

Experimenting with Events

The only way to be sure that something is working as expected is to experiment. Accordingly, you might want to add the following code to an add-in that you can tuck away somewhere for experimenting with events. The usefulness of this code is based on the use of the tool window we created for receiving messages in the client.

1. Since we will use the tool window to log messages, we suggest that you add an additional item to the Custom menu. Label the item Clear and place the following line in its Click event:

   ```
   aiMsg.Clear
   ```

2. Add the following declarations to the Connect class:

   ```
   Private WithEvents evFiles As FileControlEvents
   Private WithEvents evRefs As ReferencesEvents
   Private WithEvents evSelCtrls As SelectedVBControlsEvents
   Private WithEvents evComps As VBComponentsEvents
   Private WithEvents evCtrls As VBControlsEvents
   Private WithEvents evProjs As VBProjectsEvents
   ```

3. Add the following lines to the OnConnection event. These lines will hook events across all projects in the project group and on all forms.

   ```
   Set evFiles = _
      oVBE.Events.FileControlEvents(Nothing)

   Set evRefs = oVBE.Events.ReferencesEvents(Nothing)

   Set evSelCtrls = _
      oVBE.Events.SelectedVBControlsEvents( _
      Nothing, Nothing)

   Set evComps = _
      oVBE.Events.VBComponentsEvents(Nothing)

   Set evCtrls = oVBE.Events.VBControlsEvents( _
      Nothing, Nothing)

   Set evProjs = oVBE.Events.VBProjectsEvents()
   ```

4. Add the code shown in Example 10-1 to the Connect class. Each event is represented here, with the code required to send a message to the tool window.

Example 10-1. Methods to Add to the Connect Class

```
' File events
Private Sub evFiles_AfterAddFile( _
        ByVal VBProject As VBIDE.VBProject, _
        ByVal FileType As VBIDE.vbext_FileType, _
        ByVal FileName As String)
aiMsg.AddItem "File added: " & FileName
End Sub

Private Sub evFiles_AfterChangeFileName( _
        ByVal VBProject As VBIDE.VBProject, _
        ByVal FileType As VBIDE.vbext_FileType, _
        ByVal NewName As String, _
        ByVal OldName As String)
aiMsg.AddItem "File changed: " & OldName & " to " & NewName
End Sub

Private Sub evFiles_AfterCloseFile( _
        ByVal VBProject As VBIDE.VBProject, _
        ByVal FileType As VBIDE.vbext_FileType, _
        ByVal FileName As String, _
        ByVal WasDirty As Boolean)
aiMsg.AddItem "File closed: " & FileName & " WasDirty: " _
        & WasDirty
End Sub

Private Sub evFiles_AfterRemoveFile( _
        ByVal VBProject As VBIDE.VBProject, _
        ByVal FileType As VBIDE.vbext_FileType, _
        ByVal FileName As String)
aiMsg.AddItem "File removed: " & FileName
End Sub

Private Sub evFiles_AfterWriteFile( _
        ByVal VBProject As VBIDE.VBProject, _
        ByVal FileType As VBIDE.vbext_FileType, _
        ByVal FileName As String, _
        ByVal Result As Integer)
aiMsg.AddItem "File written to: " & FileName & " Result: " _
        & Result
End Sub

Private Sub evFiles_BeforeLoadFile( _
        ByVal VBProject As VBIDE.VBProject, _
        FileNames() As String)
If UBound(FileNames) = 1 Then
   aiMsg.AddItem "File loaded: " & FileNames(0)
ElseIf UBound(FileNames) = 2 Then
   aiMsg.AddItem "File loaded: " & FileNames(0) & " / " _
            & FileNames(1)
```

Example 10-1. Methods to Add to the Connect Class (continued)

```
End If
End Sub

Private Sub evFiles_DoGetNewFileName( _
            ByVal VBProject As VBIDE.VBProject, _
            ByVal FileType As VBIDE.vbext_FileType, _
            NewName As String, ByVal OldName As String, _
            CancelDefault As Boolean)
aiMsg.AddItem "File DoGetNewFileName: " & OldName & " to " _
              & NewName & " CancelDef: " & CancelDefault
End Sub

Private Sub evFiles_RequestChangeFileName( _
            ByVal VBProject As VBIDE.VBProject, _
            ByVal FileType As VBIDE.vbext_FileType, _
            ByVal NewName As String, _
            ByVal OldName As String, _
            Cancel As Boolean)
aiMsg.AddItem "File RequestChangeFileName: " & OldName & _
              " to " & NewName & " Cancel: " & Cancel
End Sub

Private Sub evFiles_RequestWriteFile( _
            ByVal VBProject As VBIDE.VBProject, _
            ByVal FileName As String, Cancel As Boolean)
aiMsg.AddItem "File RequestWriteName: " & FileName & _
              " Cancel: " & Cancel
End Sub

' Reference events
Private Sub evRefs_ItemAdded( _
            ByVal Reference As VBIDE.Reference)
aiMsg.AddItem "Reference added: " & Reference.Description
End Sub

Private Sub evRefs_ItemRemoved( _
            ByVal Reference As VBIDE.Reference)
aiMsg.AddItem "Reference removed: " & Reference.Description
End Sub
' Selected controls
Private Sub evSelCtrls_ItemAdded( _
            ByVal VBControl As VBIDE.VBControl)
aiMsg.AddItem "Selected control added: " & _
              VBControl.ClassName & " Name: " &
VBControl.Properties("Name").Value
End Sub

Private Sub evSelCtrls_ItemRemoved( _
            ByVal VBControl As VBIDE.VBControl)
aiMsg.AddItem "Selected control removed: " & _
              VBControl.ClassName & " Name: " & _
              VBControl.Properties("Name").Value & _
```

Example 10-1. Methods to Add to the Connect Class (continued)

```
                " / " & _
oVBE.ActiveVBProject.VBComponents("form1").Designer.SelectedVBControls.Count
End Sub

' Components
Private Sub evComps_ItemActivated( _
        ByVal VBComponent As VBIDE.VBComponent)
aiMsg.AddItem "Component activated: " & VBComponent.Name
End Sub

Private Sub evComps_ItemAdded( _
            ByVal VBComponent As VBIDE.VBComponent)
aiMsg.AddItem "Component added: " & VBComponent.Name
End Sub

Private Sub evComps_ItemReloaded(ByVal VBComponent As VBIDE.VBComponent)
aiMsg.AddItem "Component reloaded: " & VBComponent.Name
End Sub

Private Sub evComps_ItemRemoved( _
            ByVal VBComponent As VBIDE.VBComponent)
aiMsg.AddItem "Component removed: " & VBComponent.Name
End Sub

Private Sub evComps_ItemRenamed( _
        ByVal VBComponent As VBIDE.VBComponent, _
        ByVal OldName As String)
aiMsg.AddItem "Component renamed: " & OldName & " to " _
            & VBComponent.Name
End Sub

Private Sub evComps_ItemSelected( _
            ByVal VBComponent As VBIDE.VBComponent)
aiMsg.AddItem "Component selected: " & VBComponent.Name
End Sub

' Controls
Private Sub evCtrls_ItemAdded( _
            ByVal VBControl As VBIDE.VBControl)
aiMsg.AddItem "Control added: " & VBControl.ClassName _
            & " Name: " & _
            VBControl.Properties("Name").Value
End Sub

Private Sub evCtrls_ItemRemoved( _
            ByVal VBControl As VBIDE.VBControl)
aiMsg.AddItem "Control removed: " & VBControl.ClassName & _
            " Name: " & VBControl.Properties("Name").Value
End Sub

Private Sub evCtrls_ItemRenamed( _
        ByVal VBControl As VBIDE.VBControl, _
```

Example 10-1. Methods to Add to the Connect Class (continued)

```
        ByVal OldName As String, ByVal OldIndex As Long)
aiMsg.AddItem "Control renamed: " & OldName & " to " & _
     VBControl.Properties("Name").Value & " OldIndex: " & _
     OldIndex
End Sub

' Projects
Private Sub evProjs_ItemActivated( _
           ByVal VBProject As VBIDE.VBProject)
aiMsg.AddItem "Project activated: " & VBProject.Name
End Sub

Private Sub evProjs_ItemRemoved( _
           ByVal VBProject As VBIDE.VBProject)
aiMsg.AddItem "project removed " & VBProject.Name
End Sub

Private Sub evProjs_ItemAdded( _
           ByVal VBProject As VBIDE.VBProject)
aiMsg.AddItem "Project added: " & VBProject.Name
End Sub

Private Sub evProjs_ItemRenamed( _
           ByVal VBProject As VBIDE.VBProject, _
           ByVal OldName As String)
aiMsg.AddItem "Project renamed: " & OldName & " To " _
             & VBProject.Name
End Sub
```

11

Code-Related Objects

In this chapter, we take a look at the objects in the VBIDE object model that allow us to manipulate the actual code in a project. These objects are shown in Figure 11-1.

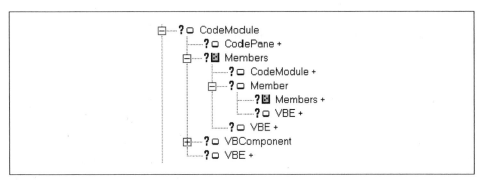

Figure 11-1. VBIDE code-related objects

The CodeModule Object

As we can see from Figure 11-1, the top-level object for code manipulation is the CodeModule object. A CodeModule object represents the code behind a VB component. Each VB component has exactly one code module.

CodeModule objects can be obtained from either a VBComponent object or a CodePane object, using each of these object's CodeModule property. (Every CodePane object is associated with a single VB component.)

Properties and Methods of the CodeModule Object

The properties and methods of the CodeModule object are shown in this list:

AddFromFile	Find	ProcCountLines
AddFromString	InsertLines	ProcOfLine
CodePane	Lines	ProcStartLine
CountOfDeclarationLines	Members	ReplaceLine
CountOfLines	Name	VBE
CreateEventProc	Parent	
DeleteLines	ProcBodyLine	

Many of these properties and methods can be grouped into some general categories as described in the following sections.

Inserting, deleting, or changing code

The following methods can insert, delete, or change existing code:

- AddFromFile method: inserts lines from a file
- AddFromString method: inserts a string
- CreateEventProc method: creates an empty event procedure
- DeleteLines method: deletes lines
- InsertLines method: inserts lines
- ReplaceLine method: replaces lines

Code statistics

The following properties can extract some statistics about a code module:

- CountOfDeclarationLines property: counts declaration lines
- CountOfLines property: counts lines in the code module
- ProcCountLines property: counts lines in a procedure

Locating code

The following members of the CodeModule object can locate and retrieve code:

- Find method: finds text
- Lines property: retrieves lines of code
- ProcBodyLine property: returns the declaration line of a procedure
- ProcOfLine property: returns the number of lines in a specified procedure
- ProcStartLine property: returns the location of the first line of a procedure

It's important to note that a procedure begins at the first line below the **End Sub**, **End Function**, or **End Property** statement of the preceding procedure. If the procedure is the first procedure, it starts at the end of the general Declarations section. Also, the last procedure in a code module includes all blank lines that follow the final **End Sub** (or **End Function** or **End Property**) statement.

Individual Members of the CodeModule Object

Let's review some of the properties and methods of the CodeModule object.

The AddFromFile method

This method inserts the contents of a text file into a code module. The syntax is:

```
CodeModuleObject.AddFromFile(filename)
```

where *filename* is the name of the file to add to the module.

Note that the AddFromFile method inserts the contents of the file starting on the line preceding the first procedure in the code module. If the module doesn't contain procedures, the contents are inserted at the end of the module.

The AddFromString method

This method adds text to a code module. The syntax is:

```
CodeModuleObject.AddFromString(stringtoadd)
```

The AddFromString method inserts the text starting on the line preceding the first procedure in the module. If the module doesn't contain procedures, the string is inserted at the end of the module.

The CodePane property

This read-only property returns the *active* CodePane object associated with the code module; that is, the code pane that would have the focus if the corresponding window also had the focus. (There may be two code panes if the window is split.)

The CountOfDeclarationLines property

This read-only property returns a Long containing the number of lines of code in the Declarations section of the code module.

The CountOfLines property

This read-only property returns a Long containing the number of lines of code in a code module. This doesn't include the last empty line that is always available in a code module.

The CreateEventProc method

This method creates an event procedure. Its syntax is:

```
CodeModuleObject.CreateEventProc(eventname, _
    objectname) As Long
```

Here, *eventname* is a string that specifies the name of the event to add to the module, and *objectname* is a string that specifies the name of the object that is the source of the event. The CreateEventProc method returns the line number of the event declaration (that is, the very first line of the event, below which is the start of the code body).

If the arguments refer to a nonexistent event, VB issues the runtime error message, "Event handler is invalid."

For instance, the code:

```
iLineNumber = oVBE.ActiveVBProject.VBComponents( _
"frmExmaple").CodeModule.CreateEventProc( _
"Click", "cmdExample")
```

creates a Click event code shell for the command button named *cmdExample* in the code module for a form named *frmExample*.

The DeleteLines method

As the name suggests, this method deletes one or more lines from a code module. The syntax is:

```
CodeModuleObject.DeleteLines(startline [, count])
```

Here *startline* is a Long that specifies the first line to delete (counting from 1), and *count* is a Long that specifies the number of lines to delete. If *count* is omitted, only one line is deleted.

The Find method

This method searches the code module for a specified string. Its syntax is:

```
CodeModuleObject.Find(target, startline, startcol, _
    endline, endcol [, wholeword] [, matchcase] _
    [, patternsearch]) As Boolean
```

The parameter *target* specifies the search string. The parameters *startline*, *endline*, *startcol*, and *endcol* are Longs that specify the search range. The last three parameters mimic the corresponding checkboxes in VB's Find dialog box. Each of the Boolean parameters is optional.

The Find method returns **True** if a match is found and **False** otherwise. Moreover, it sets *startline* to the starting line of the target (if fount). Note that setting both the *matchcase* and *patternsearch* arguments to **True** produces a runtime error. Finally, we note that the contents of the Find dialog box aren't affected by using the Find method.

The InsertLines method

This method inserts one or more lines of code at a specified location. The syntax is:

```
CodeModuleObject.InsertLines(line, code)
```

where *line* is a Long specifying the location at which to insert the code, and *code* is a String containing the code to insert. (Note that the AddFromString method is similar, but doesn't allow us to specify the location of the insertion.)

Note that the *line* argument may include the **vbCrLf** characters to create multiline insertions.

The Lines property

This property returns a String containing the specified block of lines. Its syntax is:

```
CodeModuleObject.Lines(startline As Long, _
    count As Long)
```

where *startline* is the number of the starting line to return, and *count* is the total number of lines to return.

The Members property

This property returns a Members collection. We will discuss Member objects later in the chapter.

The ProcBodyLine method

This method returns the declaration line of a procedure (the line containing the keyword **Sub**, **Function**, or **Property**). Its syntax is:

```
CodeModuleObject.ProcBodyLine( procname, prockind) _
                    As Long
```

Here, *procname* is a String containing the name of the procedure, and *prockind* specifies the type of the procedure. (The *prockind* parameter is necessary because Property procedures can have several forms: **Property Get**, **Property Let**, and **Property Set**.) In particular, the value of *prockind* is a constant from the following enum:

```
Enum vbext_ProcKind
    vbext_pk_Proc = 0
    vbext_pk_Let = 1
    vbext_pk_Set = 2
    vbext_pk_Get = 3
End Enum
```

Note that **vbext_pk_Proc** is used for all procedures other than the three types of property procedures.

The ProcCountLines method

This method returns the number of lines in a specified procedure. Its syntax is:

```
CodeModuleObject.ProcCountLines( _
    procname, prockind) As Long
```

The parameters of this method have the same meaning as those of the Proc-BodyLine method.

Note that the return value of the ProcCountLines method includes a count of all blank or comment lines immediately preceding the procedure declaration (that is, following the **End** statement in the preceding procedure). Also, if the procedure is the last procedure in a code module, the count includes any blank lines following the procedure.

The ProcOfLine method

This method returns the name of the procedure that contains a specified line. The syntax is:

```
CodeModuleObject.ProcOfLine(line, prockind) As String
```

As with the ProcBodyLine and ProcCountLines methods, we must specify the procedure kind in order to uniquely identify the procedure body.

Note that a line is within a procedure if it's a blank line or comment line preceding the procedure declaration or, if the procedure is the last procedure in a code module, a blank line following the procedure.

The ProcStartLine method

This method returns the line number of the line at which the specified procedure begins. The syntax is:

```
CodeModuleObject.ProcStartLine(procname, prockind) _
    As Long
```

Note that a procedure begins at the first line below the **End Sub** or **End Function** or **End Property** statement of the preceding procedure. If the procedure is the first procedure, it starts at the end of the general Declarations section.

The ReplaceLine method

This method replaces an existing line of code with a specified line of code. The syntax is:

```
CodeModuleObject.ReplaceLine(line, code)
```

where *line* is a Long that specifies the location of the line to replace, and *code* is a String that contains the code to insert.

The Member Object

According to the help documentation, a Member object "represents a mixture of code-based properties and type library-based attributes of members." This is certainly less than enlightening. However, Member objects can gather useful information about the members of a class module.

To get a feel for what constitutes a Member object, we consider its Type property, whose values come from the following enum:

```
Enum vbext_MemberType
    vbext_mt_Method = 1
```

```
    vbext_mt_Property = 2
    vbext_mt_Variable = 3
    vbext_mt_Event = 4
    vbext_mt_Const = 5
End Enum
```

This tells us that a Member object represents a method, property, variable, event, or constant. The following list details the properties and methods of a Member object:

Bindable	DisplayBind	StandardMethod
Browsable	HelpContextID	Static
Category	Hidden	Type
CodeLocation	Name	UIDefault
Collection	PropertyPage	VBE
DefaultBind	RequestEdit	
Description	Scope	

Unfortunately, Microsoft hasn't documented most of these properties and methods. For instance, the help documentation for the StandardMethod property says "Returns or sets the StandardMethod attribute of a Member object." This is tantamount to no documentation at all. However, we can piece together a bit of useful information on some of these items:

The Name property

Returns the name of the member.

The Scope property

Returns a constant indicating the scope of the member. Its values are taken from the following enum:

```
Enum vbext_Scope
    vbext_Private = 1
    vbext_Public = 2
    vbext_Friend = 3
End Enum
```

The Boolean Static property

Returns **True** if the member is declared as static. (This is only meaningful for variables and methods.)

The CodeLocation property

Returns the line number of the declaration of a member. For a property, this returns the line number of the **Property Get** declaration, if there is one. If not, it returns the line number of the **Property Let** or **Property Set** declaration.

Example: Pushing/Popping Prefixes

One of the most useful features of the add-in we discussed in the Preface is the feature that allows us to add or delete a prefix from selected lines of code.

The feature simply displays an input box in which to enter a string prefix. If the string begins with a hyphen, that's a signal to remove the rest of the string. The feature then simply adds or removes the string from the beginning of each selected line of code. The code is shown in Example 11-1.

Example 11-1. Code for Pushing/Popping Prefixes

```
Private Sub PushPop()

' Get the selection in the active code pane
' and append or remove a prefix

Dim i As Integer
Dim sPrefix As String
Dim fRemove As Boolean

Dim startline As Long, startcol As Long
Dim endline As Long, endcol As Long

fRemove = False
sPrefix = InputBox("Enter prefix. Precede with - to remove string.", "Push or pop
a prefix", "''")

' Check for - to signal removal
If Left$(sPrefix, 1) = "-" Then
    fRemove = True
    sPrefix = Mid$(sPrefix, 2)
End If

If sPrefix = "" Then Exit Sub

' Get startline and endline of current selection
With oVBE.ActiveCodePane

    .GetSelection startline, startcol, _
        endline, endcol

    ' If CR at end of line is selected then
    ' do not include the last line.
    If endcol = 1 Then endline = endline - 1

    With oVBE.ActiveCodePane.CodeModule
        For i = startline To endline
            If Not fRemove Then
                ' Add prefix
                .ReplaceLine i, sPrefix & .Lines(i, 1)
            Else
                ' Remove prefix if it exists
```

Example 11-1. Code for Pushing/Popping Prefixes (continued)

```
            If Left$(.Lines(i, 1), Len(sPrefix)) _
               = sPrefix Then
               .ReplaceLine i, Mid$(.Lines(i, 1), _
                 Len(sPrefix) + 1)
            End If
         End If
      Next i
   End With

   ' Shrink selection
   .SetSelection endline, 1, endline, 1

End With

End Sub
```

12

Add-in Related Objects

In this chapter, we take a look at the objects in the VB IDE object model that allow us to manipulate add-ins. These objects are shown in Figure 12-1.

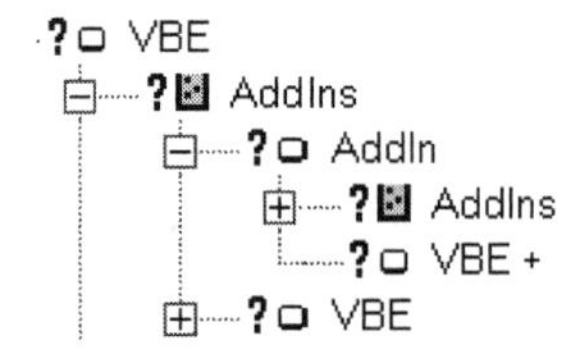

```
·?▢ VBE
    ┌──?▣ AddIns
        ┌──?▢ AddIn
            ┌──?▣ AddIns
            └──?▢ VBE +
        ┌──?▢ VBE
```

Figure 12-1. VBIDE add-in related objects

It's clear from the figure that this portion of the VBIDE model consists of two objects: the AddIn object and the corresponding AddIns collection.

Of course, an AddIn object represents a VB add-in. The AddIns collection is the collection of all add-ins that are listed in the *vbaddin.ini* file or the system registry.

The AddIn Object

The properties and methods of the AddIn object are shown in the following list:

Collection	Object
Connect	ProgId
Description	VBE
Guid	

Let's review some of these members:

The Description property

This property sets or returns a string containing the description of the add-in's Connect class (not the add-in's project description).

The Guid and Progid properties

These properties return the class ID (if the add-in is registered) and ProgID for the add-in; that is, for the Connect class of the add-in. These are the data that can be found in the system registry.

The Connect property

This Boolean property determines whether or not an add-in is connected, and to connect or disconnect the add-in. We just set the property to **True** to connect or **False** to disconnect.

Note that setting the Connect property to **True** also updates the *vbaddin.ini* file or the registry by setting the value of the ProgID for the add-in to 1. However, setting the Connect property to **False** doesn't change the *.ini* file setting to 0.

To illustrate, we can easily write an add-in that can connect and disconnect another add-in. (This is what VB's Add-In Toolbar does.) We put the following code in the Click event of a menu item:

```
Private Sub cbeCustom_Click(ByVal _
   CommandBarControl As Object, _
   handled As Boolean, CancelDefault As Boolean)

' Toggle connection for an add-in

Dim ai As VBIDE.AddIn

For Each ai In oVBE.Addins

   ' Find add-in by progID
   If ai.ProgId = "AddInTest.Connect" Then
      ai.Connect = Not ai.Connect
      ' Change menu caption
      If ai.Connect Then
         cbcCustom.Caption = "&DisconnectAITest"
      Else
         cbcCustom.Caption = "&ConnectAITest"
      End If
      Exit For
   End If

Next
' Make sure add-ins collection is up to date
oVBE.Addins.Update
End Sub
```

The AddIns Collection

This collection allows little manipulation. We can count the number of add-ins in the collection using its Count property. We can access an individual AddIn object using the (default) Item method, and we can update the collection using the Update method.

The point of the Update method is that the contents of the *vbaddin.ini* file or the add-ins defined in the registry may change. Since VB can't keep track of changes made by external sources, the Update method can refresh the AddIns collection. Incidentally, this is what occurs when the user opens the Add-In Manager dialog box.

III

Appendixes

Built-in Command Bar Controls

This appendix contains a list of built-in command bar controls, along with their ID numbers for use with the Add method of the CommandBarControls object, as discussed in Chapter 4, *Menus and Toolbars*.

Command Bar Control	ID Number	Command Bar Control	ID Number
&About Microsoft Visual Basic	927	&Delete	478
&Add Tab...	1756	&Delete Tab	1746
&Add Watch...	1820	&Delete Watch	1083
&Add-In Manager...	943	&Description	850
&Add-Ins	128	&Edit Watch...	940
&Arrange Icons	1435	&End	228
&Best of the Web	3031	&File	23
&Books Online...	2560	&Find Whole Word Only	2953
&Both	1648	&Find...	141
&Bottoms	667	&Form Layout Window	3046
&Cascade	1826	&Free Stuff	3021
&Centers	668	&Get	2647
&Clear All Bookmarks	2528	&Height	1647
&Clear All Breakpoints	579	&Help	21
&Code	2558	&Hide	865
&Copy	19	&Horizontally	1644
&Debug	511	&Immediate Window	2554
&Decrease	1649	&Increase	1650
&Decrease	1652	&Increase	1653
&Definition	939	&Indent	15

Command Bar Control	ID Number	Command Bar Control	ID Number
&Lefts	664	&Vertically	1645
&Lock Controls	519	&View	748
&Menu Editor...	474	&Web Help 14	3034
&Microsoft Visual Basic Help Topics	926	&Web Help 15	3035
		&Web Help 16	3036
&Middles	669	&Web Help 5	3025
&More Windows...	959	&Web Help 6	3026
&New Project	746	&Web Help 7	3027
&Next Bookmark	2526	&Web Help 8	3028
&Object Browser	473	&Width	1646
&Obtaining Technical Support...	815	&Window	129
		&Window Name Goes Here	830
&Options...	522	<Custom control>	1
&Order	296	A&dd Project...	3196
&Outdent	14	ActiveX Control	3050
&Paste	22	ActiveX DLL	3049
&Previous Bookmark	2527	ActiveX EXE	3048
&Product News	3022	Add &Class Module	2579
&Project Explorer	2557	Add &Form	3038
&Quick Info	2531	Add &Module	3039
&Quick Watch...	229	Add &Procedure...	559
&Recent File Name Goes Here	831	Add &Property Page	3042
&Remove	1651	Add &User Control	3041
&Remove	1654	Add ActiveX Desi&gner	166
&Rename Tab...	1878	Add MD&I Form	3040
&Restart	515	Add User &Document	3044
&Rights	665	Brea&k	189
&Run	4	C&heck Out	1718
&Run To Cursor	1811	Check &In	1717
&Start	186	Co&llapse Parent	725
&Toggle	293	Color Pa&lette	207
&Toggle Bookmark	2525	Comment Block	192
&Toggle Breakpoint	51	Complete &Word	2533
&Toolbars	167	Find &Next	570
&Tools	752	For &Developers Only Home Page	3029
&Tops	666		
&Undo Check Out	2650	Frequently Asked &Questions	3023

Command Bar Control	ID Number	Command Bar Control	ID Number
He&lp	49	S&plit	302
Help	620	Sav&e Project As...	749
Insert Fi&le...	1400	Search the &Web...	3032
Last Positio&n	1822	Select &All	756
Li&st Constants	2530	Send Feedbac&k...	3030
List Properties/Met&hods	2529	Set &Next Statement	1812
Local&s Window	2555	Set as Start &Up	1821
Make &Equal	408	Show &Hidden Members	2689
Make &Equal	465	Show Ne&xt Statement	1813
Microsoft &Home Page	3091	Size to Gri&d	550
Microsoft on the &Web	549	Standard EXE	3047
O&bject	2553	Step &Into	188
Online &Support	3024	Step &Over	194
Para&meter Info	2532	Step O&ut	2559
Paste Lin&k	755	Tile &Horizontally	2562
Project Window Related Documents Folder	512	Tile &Vertically	2561
		to &Grid	573
Project1 Prop&erties...	2578	Toggle Folders	32
Properties &Window	222	Toolbo&x	548
Property Pa&ges	3045	Uncomment Block	2552
R&eplace...	313	View &Definition	2690
Refere&nces...	942	Watc&h Window	2556
Resolution &Guides	520	Web &Tutorial	3033

B

Face IDs

The FaceID property of a CommandBarButton object defines the icon that's displayed on the button's face. (For an example of using the FaceID property to define the image on a button's face, see the section "Example: Creating a Toolbar," in Chapter 4, *Menus and Toolbars.*)

Figures B-1 through B-5 show each of the icons that are available from Visual Basic, along with their corresponding faceIDs. Each figure shows 400 icons whose beginning and ending faceIDs are shown in the figure caption of the image. In addition, to make identifying a particular faceID easier, a numbered grid has been superimposed on the image. The column numbers indicate the one's digit; the row numbers indicate all other significant digits. For example, the faceID of the F icon in Figure B-1 is 85, because it's in row 8x (the row containing faceIDs 80–89) and in column x5 (the column containing faceIDs whose one's digit is 5).

Note that some numbers aren't used as faceIDs; in these cases, no icon is displayed in that faceID's grid in Figures B-1 through B-5.

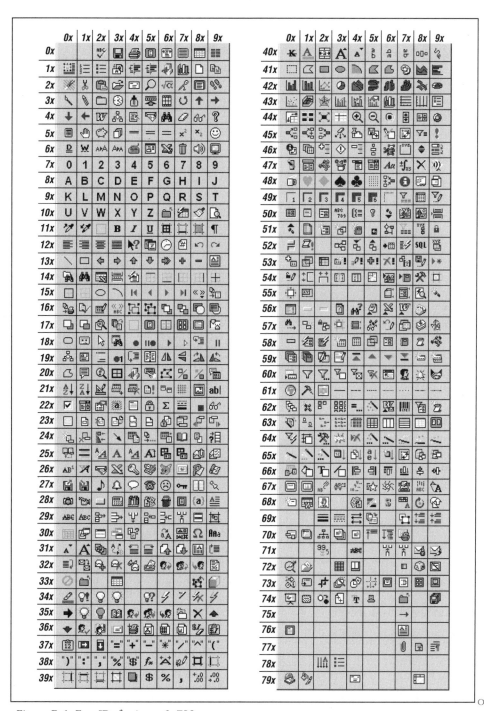

Figure B-1. FaceIDs for icons 0–799

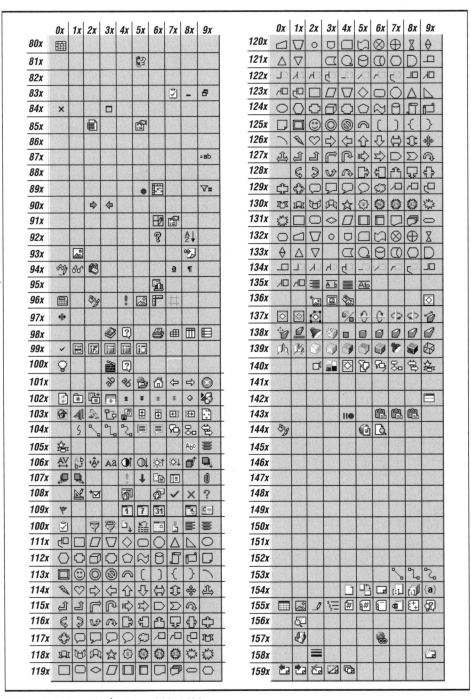

Figure B-2. FaceIDs for icons 800–1599

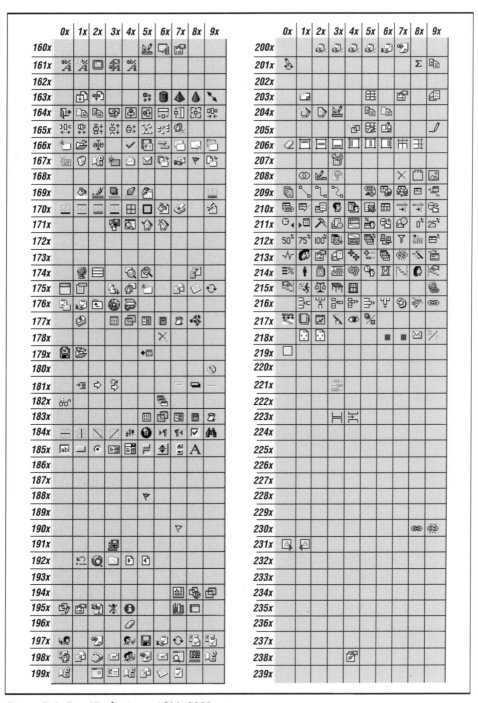

Figure B-3. FaceIDs for icons 1600–2399

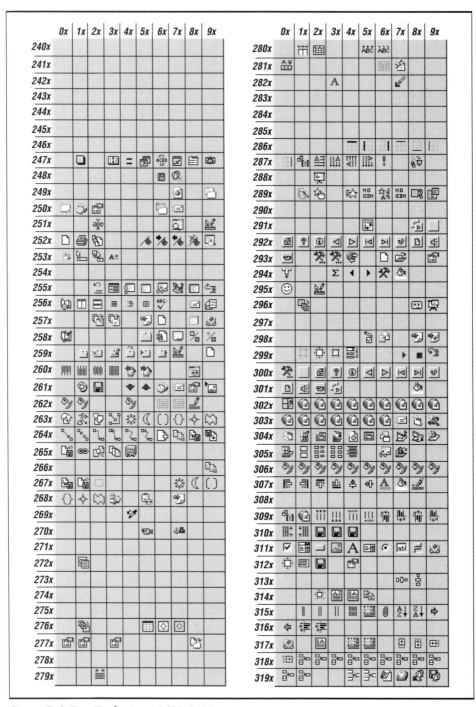

Figure B-4. FaceIDs for icons 2400–3199

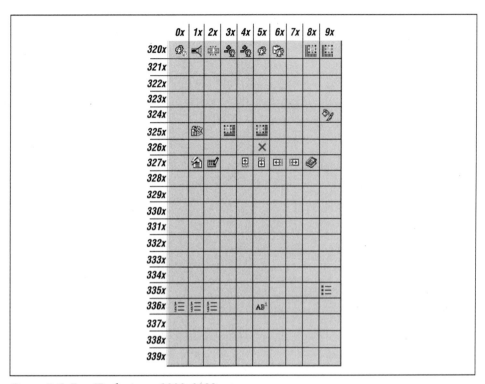

Figure B-5. FaceIDs for icons 3200–3399

Index

About the Author

Steven Roman is a professor of Mathematics at the California State University, Fullerton. He has taught at a number of other universities, including MIT, the University of California at Santa Barbara, and the University of South Florida. Dr. Roman received his B.A. degree from the University of California at Los Angeles and his Ph.D. from the University of Washington. Dr. Roman has authored 31 books, including a number of books on mathematics, such as *Coding and Information Theory, Advanced Linear Algebra,* and *Field Theory,* published by Springer-Verlag. He has also written a series of 15 small books entitled *Modules in Mathematics,* designed for the general college-level liberal arts student. Dr. Roman has written *Learning Word Programming* and *Access Database Design and Programming* for O'Reilly & Associates, and two other computer books, entitled *Concepts of Object-Oriented Programming with Visual Basic,* published by Springer-Verlag, and *Understanding Personal Computer Hardware,* an in-depth look at how PC hardware works (no publisher yet). Dr. Roman is interested in combinatorics, algebra, and computer science.

Colophon

The bird on the cover of *Developing Visual Basic Add-ins* is a jacana, a tropical wading bird. There are eight species of jacana, in six genera. The jacana's most remarkable physical characteristic is its long toes. In fact, the jacana has the longest toes (relatively speaking) of any living bird. When in flight, the toes extend beyond the tip of the bird's tail. These long, wide-spread toes enable the jacana to walk across the floating leaves of water plants, hence the names lotus bird and lily trotter, by which some species of jacana are known. As useful as they are when walking on watery surfaces, the jacana's toes make walking on land very difficult, and for this reason you rarely see a jacana walking on solid ground. For that matter, most of you will rarely see a jacana, as very few of them are found in captivity. They can be found in fresh-water ponds and swamps in tropical regions throughout the world. Jacanas feed mainly on insects, small mollusks, and small fish.

Jacana females are frequently larger than the males and more aggressive. In most jacana species, the female mates with more than one male and lays more than one clutch of eggs per season. There are typically four glossy, "scribbled" eggs per clutch, laid in nests that float on the water. The male incubates the eggs and raises the young alone. Jacana chicks can swim and dive immediately after hatching. The father doesn't feed the young, as they are able to find and digest their own food, but he does protect and comfort them for the first few months of life.

Mary Anne Weeks Mayo was the project manager and copyeditor for *Developing Visual Basic Add-ins*; Jane Ellin, Melanie Wang, Sarah Jane Shangraw, and Sheryl Avruch reviewed the book for quality control; Ruth Rautenberg wrote the index; and Kathleen Wilson created the back cover.

Edie Freedman designed the cover of this book using a 19th-century engraving from the Dover Pictorial Archive. The cover layout was produced with Quark-XPress 3.32 using the ITC Garamond font. Whenever possible, our books use RepKover™, a durable and flexible lay-flat binding. If the page count exceeds RepKover's limit, perfect binding is used.

The inside layout was designed by Nancy Priest and implemented in FrameMaker by Mike Sierra. The text and heading fonts are ITC Garamond Light and Garamond Book. The illustrations that appear in the book were created in Macromedia Freehand 8 and screen shots were created in Adobe Photoshop 5 by Robert Romano. This colophon was written by Clairemarie Fisher O'Leary.

More Titles from O'Reilly

Windows Programming

Access Database Design & Programming

By Steven Roman
1st Edition June 1997
270 pages, ISBN 1-56592-297-2

This book provides experienced Access users who are novice programers with frequently overlooked concepts and techniques necessary to create effective database applications. It focuses on designing effective tables in a multi-table application; using the Access interface or Access SQL to construct queries; and programming using the Data Access Object (DAO) and Microsoft Access object models.

VB & VBA in a Nutshell: The Languages

By Paul Lomax
1st Edition October 1998
656 pages, ISBN 1-56592-358-8

For Visual Basic and VBA programmers, this book boils down the essentials of the VB and VBA languages into a single volume, including undocumented and little documented areas essential to everyday programming. The convenient alphabetical reference to all functions, procedures, statements, and keywords allows VB and VBA programmers to use this book both as a standard reference guide to the language and as a tool for troubleshooting and identifying programming problems.

Learning VBScript

By Paul Lomax
1st Edition July 1997
616 pages, includes CD-ROM
ISBN 1-56592-247-6

This definitive guide shows web developers how to take full advantage of client-side scripting with the VBScript language. In addition to basic language features, it covers the Internet Explorer object model and discusses techniques for client-side scripting, like adding ActiveX controls to a web page or validating data before sending it to the server. Includes CD-ROM with over 170 code samples.

Visual Basic Controls in a Nutshell

By Evan S. Dictor
1st Edition March 1999 (est.)
522 pages (est.), ISBN 1-56592-294-8

This quick reference covers one of the crucial elements of Visual Basic: its controls, and their numerous properties, events, and methods. It provides a step-by-step list of procedures for using each major control and contains a detailed reference to all properties, methods, and events. Written by an experienced Visual Basic programmer, it helps to make painless what can sometimes be an arduous job of programming Visual Basic.

Learning Perl on Win32 Systems

By Randal L. Schwartz,
Erik Olson & Tom Christiansen
1st Edition August 1997
306 pages, ISBN 1-56592-324-3

In this carefully paced course, leading Perl trainers and a Windows NT practitioner teach you to program in the language that promises to emerge as the scripting language of choice on NT. Based on the "llama" book, this book features tips for PC users and new, NT-specific examples, along with a foreword by Larry Wall, the creator of Perl, and Dick Hardt, the creator of Perl for Win32.

Learning Word Programming

By Steven Roman
1st Edition October 1998
408 pages, ISBN 1-56592-524-6

This no-nonsense book delves into the core aspects of VBA programming, enabling users to increase their productivity and power over Microsoft Word. It takes the reader step-by-step through writing VBA macros and programs, illustrating how to generate tables of a particular format, manage shortcut keys, create FAX cover sheets, and reformat documents.

O'REILLY®

TO ORDER: **800-998-9938** • *order@oreilly.com* • *http://www.oreilly.com/*
OUR PRODUCTS ARE AVAILABLE AT A BOOKSTORE OR SOFTWARE STORE NEAR YOU.
FOR INFORMATION: **800-998-9938** • **707-829-0515** • *info@oreilly.com*

Windows Programming

Developing Windows Error Messages

By Ben Ezzell
1st Edition March 1998
254 pages, Includes CD-ROM
ISBN 1-56592-356-1

This book teaches C, C++, and Visual Basic programmers how to write effective error messages that notify the user of an error, clearly explain the error, and most important, offer a solution. The book also discusses methods for preventing and trapping errors before they occur and tells how to create flexible input and response routines to keep unnecessary errors from happening.

Inside the Windows 95 File System

By Stan Mitchell
1st Edition May 1997
378 pages, Includes diskette
ISBN 1-56592-200-X

In this book, Stan Mitchell describes the Windows 95 File System, as well as the new opportunities and challenges it brings for developers. Its "hands-on" approach will help developers become better equipped to make design decisions using the new Win95 File System features. Includes a diskette containing MULTIMON, a general-purpose monitor for examining Windows internals.

Win32 Multithreaded Programming

By Aaron Cohen & Mike Woodring
1st Edition December 1997
724 pages, Includes CD-ROM
ISBN 1-56592-296-4

This book clearly explains the concepts of multithreaded programs and shows developers how to construct efficient and complex applications. An important book for any developer, it illustrates all aspects of Win32 multithreaded programming, including what has previously been undocumented or poorly explained.

Windows NT File System Internals

By Rajeev Nagar
1st Edition September 1997
794 pages, Includes diskette
ISBN 1-56592-249-2

Windows NT File System Internals presents the details of the NT I/O Manager, the Cache Manager, and the Memory Manager from the perspective of a software developer writing a file system driver or implementing a kernel-mode filter driver. The book provides numerous code examples included on diskette, as well as the source for a complete, usable filter driver.

Inside the Windows 95 Registry

By Ron Petrusha
1st Edition August 1996
594 pages, Includes diskette
ISBN 1-56592-170-4

An in-depth examination of remote registry access, differences between the Win95 and NT registries, registry backup, undocumented registry services, and the role the registry plays in OLE. Shows programmers how to access the Win95 registry from Win32, Win16, and DOS programs in C and Visual Basic. VxD sample code is also included. Includes diskette.

Windows NT SNMP

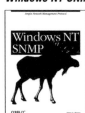

By James D. Murray
1st Edition January 1998
464 pages, Includes CD-ROM
ISBN 1-56592-338-3

This book describes the implementation of SNMP (the Simple Network Management Protocol) on Windows NT 3.51 and 4.0 (with a look ahead to NT 5.0) and Windows 95 systems. It covers SNMP and network basics and detailed information on developing SNMP management applications and extension agents. The book comes with a CD-ROM containing a wealth of additional information: standards documents, sample code from the book, and many third-party, SNMP-related software tools, libraries, and demos.

Web Programming

CGI Programming on the World Wide Web

By Shishir Gundavaram
1st Edition March 1996
450 pages, ISBN 1-56592-168-2

This book offers a comprehensive explanation of CGI and related techniques for people who hold on to the dream of providing their own information servers on the Web. It starts at the beginning, explaining the value of CGI and how it works, then moves swiftly into the subtle details of programming.

Dynamic HTML: The Definitive Reference

By Danny Goodman
1st Edition July 1998
1088 pages, ISBN 1-56592-494-0

Dynamic HTML: The Definitive Reference is an indispensable compendium for Web content developers. It contains complete reference material for all of the HTML tags, CSS style attributes, browser document objects, and JavaScript objects supported by the various standards and the latest versions of Netscape Navigator and Microsoft Internet Explorer.

Frontier: The Definitive Guide

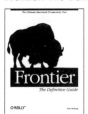

By Matt Neuburg
1st Edition February 1998
618 pages, 1-56592-383-9

This definitive guide is the first book devoted exclusively to teaching and documenting Userland Frontier, a powerful scripting environment for web site management and system level scripting. Packed with examples, advice, tricks, and tips, *Frontier: The Definitive Guide* teaches you Frontier from the ground up. Learn how to automate repetitive processes, control remote computers across a network, beef up your web site by generating hundreds of related web pages automatically, and more. Covers Frontier 4.2.3 for the Macintosh.

JavaScript: The Definitive Guide, 3rd Edition

By David Flanagan & Dan Shafer
3rd Edition June 1998
800 pages, ISBN 1-56592-392-8

This third edition of the definitive reference to JavaScript covers the latest version of the language, JavaScript 1.2, as supported by Netscape Navigator 4.0. JavaScript, which is being standardized under the name ECMAScript, is a scripting language that can be embedded directly in HTML to give web pages programming-language capabilities.

Web Client Programming with Perl

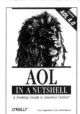

By Clinton Wong
1st Edition March 1997
228 pages, ISBN 1-56592-214-X

Web Client Programming with Perl shows you how to extend scripting skills to the Web. This book teaches you the basics of how browsers communicate with servers and how to write your own customized web clients to automate common tasks. It is intended for those who are motivated to develop software that offers a more flexible and dynamic response than a standard web browser.

In a Nutshell Quick References

AOL in a Nutshell

By Curt Degenhart & Jen Muehlbauer
1st Edition June 1998
536 pages, ISBN 1-56592-424-X

This definitive reference breaks through the hype and shows advanced AOL users and sophisticated beginners how to get the most out of AOL's tools and features. You'll learn how to customize AOL to meet your needs, work around annoying idiosyncrasies, avoid unwanted email and Instant Messages, understand Parental Controls, and turn off intrusive advertisements. It's an indispensable guide for users who aren't dummies.

In a Nutshell Quick References

Internet in a Nutshell

By Valerie Quercia
1st Edition October 1997
450 pages, ISBN 1-56592-323-5

Internet in a Nutshell is a quick-moving guide that goes beyond the "hype" and right to the heart of the matter: how to get the Internet to work for you. This is a second-generation Internet book for readers who have already taken a spin around the Net and now want to learn the shortcuts.

ASP in a Nutshell

By A. Keyton Weissinger
1st Edition February 1999 (est.)
300 pages (est.), ISBN 1-56592-490-8

This detailed reference contains all the information Web developers need to create effective Active Server Pages (ASP) applications. It focuses on how features are used in a real application and highlights little-known or undocumented aspects, enabling even experienced developers to advance their ASP applications to new levels.

WebMaster in a Nutshell

By Stephen Spainhour & Valerie Quercia
1st Edition October 1996
374 pages, ISBN 1-56592-229-8

Web content providers and administrators have many sources for information, both in print and online. *WebMaster in a Nutshell* puts it all together in one slim volume for easy desktop access. This quick reference covers HTML, CGI, JavaScript, Perl, HTTP, and server configuration.

Web Design in a Nutshell

By Jennifer Niederst
1st Edition November 1998 (est.)
580 pages (est.), ISBN 1-56592-515-7

Web Design in a Nutshell contains the nitty-gritty on everything you need to know to design Web pages. Written by veteran Web designer Jennifer Niederst, this book provides quick access to the wide range of technologies and techniques from which Web designers and authors must draw. Topics include understanding the Web environment, HTML, graphics, multimedia and interactivity, and emerging technologies.

WebMaster in a Nutshell, Deluxe Edition

By O'Reilly & Associates, Inc.
1st Edition September 1997
374 pages, includes CD-ROM & book
ISBN 1-56592-305-7

The Deluxe Edition of *WebMaster in a Nutshell* is a complete library for web programmers. It features the Web Developer's Library, a CD-ROM containing the electronic text of five popular O'Reilly titles: *HTML: The Definitive Guide*, 2nd Edition; *JavaScript: The Definitive Guide*, 2nd Edition; *CGI Programming on the World Wide Web*; *Programming Perl*, 2nd Edition—the classic "camel book"; and *WebMaster in a Nutshell*, which is also included in a companion desktop edition.

Perl in a Nutshell

By Stephen Spainhour, Ellen Siever & Nathan Patwardhan
1st Edition December 1998 (est.)
544 pages (est.), ISBN 1-56592-286-7

The perfect companion for working programmers, *Perl in a Nutshell* is a comprehensive reference guide to the world of Perl. It contains everything you need to know for all but the most obscure Perl questions. This wealth of information is packed into an efficient, extraordinarily usable format.

O'REILLY®

TO ORDER: **800-998-9938** • *order@oreilly.com* • *http://www.oreilly.com/*
OUR PRODUCTS ARE AVAILABLE AT A BOOKSTORE OR SOFTWARE STORE NEAR YOU.
FOR INFORMATION: **800-998-9938** • **707-829-0515** • *info@oreilly.com*

How to stay in touch with O'Reilly

1. Visit Our Award-Winning Web Site

http://www.oreilly.com/

★ "Top 100 Sites on the Web" —*PC Magazine*
★ "Top 5% Web sites" —*Point Communications*
★ "3-Star site" — *The McKinley Group*

Our web site contains a library of comprehensive product information (including book excerpts and tables of contents), downloadable software, background articles, interviews with technology leaders, links to relevant sites, book cover art, and more. File us in your Bookmarks or Hotlist!

2. Join Our Email Mailing Lists

New Product Releases

To receive automatic email with brief descriptions of all new O'Reilly products as they are released, send email to:
listproc@online.oreilly.com
Put the following information in the first line of your message (*not* in the Subject field):
subscribe oreilly-news

O'Reilly Events

If you'd also like us to send information about trade show events, special promotions, and other O'Reilly events, send email to:
listproc@online.oreilly.com
Put the following information in the first line of your message (*not* in the Subject field):
subscribe oreilly-events

3. Get Examples from Our Books via FTP

There are two ways to access an archive of example files from our books:

Regular FTP

- ftp to:
  ftp.oreilly.com
  (login: anonymous
  password: your email address)
- Point your web browser to:
  ftp://ftp.oreilly.com/

FTPMAIL

- Send an email message to:
  ftpmail@online.oreilly.com
  (Write "help" in the message body)

4. Contact Us via Email

order@oreilly.com
To place a book or software order online. Good for North American and international customers.

subscriptions@oreilly.com
To place an order for any of our newsletters or periodicals.

books@oreilly.com
General questions about any of our books.

software@oreilly.com
For general questions and product information about our software. Check out O'Reilly Software Online at **http://software.oreilly.com/** for software and technical support information. Registered O'Reilly software users send your questions to: **website-support@oreilly.com**

cs@oreilly.com
For answers to problems regarding your order or our products.

booktech@oreilly.com
For book content technical questions or corrections.

proposals@oreilly.com
To submit new book or software proposals to our editors and product managers.

international@oreilly.com
For information about our international distributors or translation queries. For a list of our distributors outside of North America check out:
http://www.oreilly.com/www/order/country.html

O'Reilly & Associates, Inc.
101 Morris Street, Sebastopol, CA 95472 USA
TEL   707-829-0515 or 800-998-9938
          (6am to 5pm PST)
FAX   707-829-0104

International Distributors

UK, Europe, Middle East and Northern Africa (except France, Germany, Switzerland, & Austria)

INQUIRIES

International Thomson Publishing Europe
Berkshire House
168-173 High Holborn
London WC1V 7AA
United Kingdom
Telephone: 44-171-497-1422
Fax: 44-171-497-1426
Email: itpint@itps.co.uk

ORDERS

International Thomson Publishing Services, Ltd.
Cheriton House, North Way
Andover, Hampshire SP10 5BE
United Kingdom
Telephone: 44-264-342-832 (UK)
Telephone: 44-264-342-806 (outside UK)
Fax: 44-264-364418 (UK)
Fax: 44-264-342761 (outside UK)
UK & Eire orders: itpuk@itps.co.uk
International orders: itpint@itps.co.uk

France

Editions Eyrolles
61 bd Saint-Germain
75240 Paris Cedex 05
France
Fax: 33-01-44-41-11-44

FRENCH LANGUAGE BOOKS

All countries except Canada
Telephone: 33-01-44-41-46-16
Email: geodif@eyrolles.com
English language books
Telephone: 33-01-44-41-11-87
Email: distribution@eyrolles.com

Germany, Switzerland, and Austria

INQUIRIES

O'Reilly Verlag
Balthasarstr. 81
D-50670 Köln
Germany
Telephone: 49-221-97-31-60-0
Fax: 49-221-97-31-60-8
Email: anfragen@oreilly.de

ORDERS

International Thomson Publishing
Königswinterer Straße 418
53227 Bonn, Germany
Telephone: 49-228-97024 0
Fax: 49-228-441342
Email: order@oreilly.de

Japan

O'Reilly Japan, Inc.
Kiyoshige Building 2F
12-Banchi, Sanei-cho
Shinjuku-ku
Tokyo 160-0008 Japan
Telephone: 81-3-3356-5227
Fax: 81-3-3356-5261
Email: kenji@oreilly.com

India

Computer Bookshop (India) PVT. Ltd.
190 Dr. D.N. Road, Fort
Bombay 400 001 India
Telephone: 91-22-207-0989
Fax: 91-22-262-3551
Email: cbsbom@giasbm01.vsnl.net.in

Hong Kong

City Discount Subscription Service Ltd.
Unit D, 3rd Floor, Yan's Tower
27 Wong Chuk Hang Road
Aberdeen, Hong Kong
Telephone: 852-2580-3539
Fax: 852-2580-6463
Email: citydis@ppn.com.hk

Korea

Hanbit Media, Inc.
Sonyoung Bldg. 202
Yeksam-dong 736-36
Kangnam-ku
Seoul, Korea
Telephone: 822-554-9610
Fax: 822-556-0363
Email: hant93@chollian.dacom.co.kr

Singapore, Malaysia, and Thailand

Addison Wesley Longman Singapore PTE Ltd.
25 First Lok Yang Road
Singapore 629734
Telephone: 65-268-2666
Fax: 65-268-7023
Email: daniel@longman.com.sg

Philippines

Mutual Books, Inc.
429-D Shaw Boulevard
Mandaluyong City, Metro
Manila, Philippines
Telephone: 632-725-7538
Fax: 632-721-3056
Email: mbikikog@mnl.sequel.net

China

Ron's DataCom Co., Ltd.
79 Dongwu Avenue
Dongxihu District
Wuhan 430040
China
Telephone: 86-27-83892568
Fax: 86-27-83222108
Email: hongfeng@public.wh.hb.cn

All Other Asian Countries

O'Reilly & Associates, Inc.
101 Morris Street
Sebastopol, CA 95472 USA
Telephone: 707-829-0515
Fax: 707-829-0104
Email: order@oreilly.com

Australia

WoodsLane Pty. Ltd.
7/5 Vuko Place, Warriewood NSW 2102
P.O. Box 935
Mona Vale NSW 2103
Australia
Telephone: 61-2-9970-5111
Fax: 61-2-9970-5002
Email: info@woodslane.com.au

New Zealand

Woodslane New Zealand Ltd.
21 Cooks Street (P.O. Box 575)
Waganui, New Zealand
Telephone: 64-6-347-6543
Fax: 64-6-345-4840
Email: info@woodslane.com.au

The Americas

McGraw-Hill Interamericana Editores, S.A. de C.V.
Cedro No. 512
Col. Atlampa 06450
Mexico, D.F.
Telephone: 52-5-541-3155
Fax: 52-5-541-4913
Email: mcgraw-hill@infosel.net.mx

South Africa

International Thomson Publishing South Africa
Building 18, Constantia Park
138 Sixteenth Road
P.O. Box 2459
Halfway House, 1685 South Africa
Telephone: 27-11-805-4819
Fax: 27-11-805-3648

O'REILLY®